AANIKA GAJENDRAGAD

Chennai • Bangalore

CLEVER FOX PUBLISHING
Chennai, India

Published by CLEVER FOX PUBLISHING 2024
Copyright © Aanika Gajendragad 2024

All Rights Reserved.
ISBN: 978-93-56488-07-6

This book has been published with all reasonable efforts taken to make the material error-free after the consent of the author. No part of this book shall be used, reproduced in any manner whatsoever without written permission from the author, except in the case of brief quotations embodied in critical articles and reviews.

The Author of this book is solely responsible and liable for its content including but not limited to the views, representations, descriptions, statements, information, opinions and references ["Content"]. The Content of this book shall not constitute or be construed or deemed to reflect the opinion or expression of the Publisher or Editor. Neither the Publisher nor Editor endorse or approve the Content of this book or guarantee the reliability, accuracy or completeness of the Content published herein and do not make any representations or warranties of any kind, express or implied, including but not limited to the implied warranties of merchantability, fitness for a particular purpose. The Publisher and Editor shall not be liable whatsoever for any errors, omissions, whether such errors or omissions result from negligence, accident, or any other cause or claims for loss or damages of any kind, including without limitation, indirect or consequential loss or damage arising out of use, inability to use, or about the reliability, accuracy or sufficiency of the information contained in this book.

FOREWORD

These days, you won't find too many 16-year-olds who love reading books, let alone write one. This says a lot about Aanika and her passion; a true aberration. Let me tell you a bit more since I am totally stupefied by her.

The modern day has sucked out a lot of the joys that we associate with childhood and growing up years. The rat race starts way too early. The academic burdens are way too excessive. The social pressures are way too much. The social media distractions are way too magnetic. So, here's the first thing that stumped me about Aanika, as also her parents. At such an early age, how did she decide to sidestep the regular world and become an earnest writer?

After all, writing requires passion, patience, understanding of (and exposure to) life, language, curiosity, craft, clarity of thought, imagination, intelligence, a sense of structure, sensitivity etc. Beyond all that, here's the hard reality:

Writing is the loneliest profession that I can think of. It's just You Vs The Blank Page.

The fact that Aanika has chosen this since she was nine is stupendous. The fact that she has already published over 20 short stories and penned two full-length novels … even more so. The almost-unthinkable act of dropping out of school (and getting home-schooled) so that she could spend more time writing raised my eyebrows, which remained raised for a while. It is fairly common for sportspeople to find their calling at a tender age but a young girl wanting to be a serious writer?

Hmmm!

Now, let me come to the real deal: her writing.

For someone so young, she has vivid imagination and a vocabulary to match. She creates her world and characters with depth and definition. She is blessed with the ability to draw from her own life, the lives around her, and from what she's heard, seen and read about. She has the innate knack of infusing drama without which any story turns into mere words across several pages.

Aanika is a new, young voice in literature that you should hear.

More than anything, a writer needs three things – a small space, a big mind and a bigger heart. I wish you all of them. Congratulations, Aanika. God bless you!

– Anand Suspi
(Author of Half Pants Full Pants & The Bookseller of Mogga)

AUTHOR NOTE

To whoever reads this part of the book; thank you for not skipping! I believe I spent more than a year working on this book and it was absolutely challenging. More so because I reworked this plot I had published on an online platform in a shorter format years ago. Nevertheless, it holds a special place in my heart, because that's when I decided that I really want to do this. Become an author. Write stories for the rest of my life. That's when I continued my studies by means of homeschooling. That way I got enough time to write and focus on what I enjoyed, rather than being stuck in the "traffic" of the rat race. That exact storyline is the reason I'm writing this today, no matter how cheesy the first book was. As I present this book, I'd like to acknowledge a few people. My older sister Advika, the one who inspired me to build a passion in life. Writing to me is like cooking to her. She is also the one who designed the book cover. Pappa, Amma and Asmita Aunty, thank you for always encouraging me in life, for not letting me get sidetracked from my goals and for supporting me throughout my journey of writing this book. To my family and friends, for always being there for me. To the publishing team of CleverFox, thank you for this!

I hope you'll enjoy reading this book as much as I did while writing it. If you are a young adult, may it inspire you to follow your passion. For the older readers, I hope you'll consider encouraging your younger ones to pursue their dreams.

*– **Aanika***
Bangalore,
July 2024

Chapter 1

I was doomed. Gone. No, really. I was stranded in Australia with very few dollars to keep me going. Okay, maybe 'being stranded' was an over-exaggeration. It was my choice, after all. A choice I was beginning to regret.

Fine. Jokes apart, (yes, I was joking. I make unfunny jokes when I'm stressed.) I actually felt a lot freer. Like as though I was a bird locked in a cage before. Technically, I was.

I was living in a fairy tale. Rapunzel's. I was Rapunzel, my parents the evil old witch(es). All that time, it seemed like I was waiting for my own Flynn Rider to come along and save me from there.

This was not an exaggeration. They were both self-centred and big people pleasers. If anyone would want to spend a day with them… no, they wouldn't want to.

I had done limited research. I knew I should have done more. If only the man sitting next to me on the flight wasn't a 'let-things-go-the-way-they're-supposed-to' guy. I should've listened to the old woman instead, who was eavesdropping on our conversation and mumbling to herself. "This generation is done for," she had said in her posh British accent. "Billy- don't let them influence you when you get older." I could swear I saw the baby on her lap nod its head.

I couldn't believe this. I had a house. A real one, not the one I used to play with while being trapped in the towers as Rapunzel. I ran to some people asking for help and they showed me the way to a real estate office situated right next to the airport. The house was small, dusty but I could deal with it.

The first thing I did was introduce myself to my lovely neighbours. On one side was a house covered with creepers and pretty purple flowers, on the other a vintage-like house, brown and white in colour. The houses pretty much defined the people residing in them…well, that was going by what I understood about them from our first meeting.

In the house with the flowers lived a middle-aged woman– about 50 in age– with a bright personality. She seemed like someone who would bake cookies and hand them to the entire neighbourhood or someone who would invite everyone home for a big meal. I definitely did not think she was the type to attend parties, but she surprised me. "It's no small party, dear. It's the town's biggest party held every year," Mrs Jones explained. She told me I would meet people "of my lot" at the party if I came. I assumed she meant *Indians*. "You're going to love it there, *Barkha*, trust me. It's a great opportunity to meet people," she spoke over a cup of tea. I was sure she meant that with good intentions and tried hard not to be… a racist.

The other house bore an old man. He held a brown cane to support his walking, but unlike his appearance, he was somewhat active. And I knew this only because I caught him turning off his 'daily Zumba class' – as the screen read. Mr. Thomas, or Philip, seemed pretty embarrassed when he turned the television off.

"Ah- hello, sweet girl. May I ask you your name?" His British accent was very strong. When I pointed that out to him, he flashed me the widest smile. He went on about how he existed during the Second World War – how where he lived was almost destroyed causing him and his late wife (may she rest in peace) to shift to the town. His wife was a very humble woman. A sad death she had. Sad yet peaceful, according to him. She was super excited for her grandchildren to show up all the way from the United States but unfortunately passed away in her sleep the night before. What was supposed to be a happy vacation away from home for the children turned out to be a mourning period. They came to have fun but ended with a *fun*eral instead.

When I got back home (wow that felt nice to say- home), I thought about the party Mrs Jones had mentioned. What was surprising was the fact that it was literally that night. The night I arrived. Call it a coincidence, I would call it destiny. This town was meant to be lived in by me. It was fate.

But then again, would attending this party really be helpful? Sure, I would be meeting new people. That was the main thing, right? Also the worst thing. I would, again, blame my parents for not letting me socialize. "Study, then go out," they preached. And then wouldn't let me go out after I was done studying.

Back at my parent's house, I used to count the number of seconds the clouds in the sky took to pass the big window in my room. On good days, the clouds moved fast. Good days meant the days my parents were in a good mood. I had come to realise that the clouds moved slowly on bad days only. The students that sat next to me at school would look at me weirdly if I mentioned the clouds' speed out of nowhere.

The clouds were fast on the first day I moved to Australia. It was a sign. I observed when I walked to the nearest grocery market for lunch.

Chapter 2

Okay, question. Would one rather prefer to eat something you're very used to, or try something they had never heard of? On a lazy day? Let me rephrase that. Would they rather eat hot, soupy, delicious instant cup noodles, or *damper*- which I didn't even know was a thing? It was bread with salt– I got to know about it only after looking it up on Google. I got that trying things (especially food) was super fun. I really needed to stay at home and rest, though. I wished the seller on the street would understand that…because he was following me until I reached the store and got in. He got salty with me. He was a salty man selling salty slices of bread.

Fifty Australian dollars. That was all I had. How was I going to survive until I finished writing the book? Even after I did, what if no one was willing to publish it? Why had I not thought of it before I actually travelled all the way there?

I sighed in regret as I left the store. But wait—

Not two seconds later, I scrambled back into the place. On the white and yellow wall was a noticeboard. A small sign on it read, 'Hiring!'.

"Please, please, please," I prayed and walked to the blond guy behind the billing counter. He stood nonchalantly, resting his body on the counter. Only when I approached him, I noticed him talking to a brunette. She had her hair in a fancy bun and wore luxury brand clothes. I wore a plaid shirt with blue jeans. Talk about contrast.

"Excuse me- oh, I'm sorry, was I interrupting something?" I spoke. The two turned their heads at me, one very smiley and the other very noticeably judging.

"No, you weren't. Did you forget something?" The man asked. His greyish-black eyes glistened at me.

"I just wanted to know if you were hiring. Because the sign said—"

"The sign," he interrupted, exhaling. "I told you the right person would see it!" He said to the lady.

She dismissed him with her hand. I then observed that her eyes had never left me. She seemed somewhat intrigued like I was a different creature altogether.

"Where do you live?" she asked me. She was Indian, I just knew from her face. However, she spoke with an Australian accent.

"Oh, I don't really know the address, but it's on the next street. I moved in just this morning, so…"

"Next street?!" The boy shrieked. "That's like almost half an hour away!"

I shrugged. "It barely took me ten minutes to walk."

"You walked?" They both looked at me in disbelief— which I didn't get why. What was so surprising about it? Did Australia and India have different speeds and distances?

"You're hired," the other Indian said to me almost instantly. "I'll lend you one of my father's cars first thing tomorrow. Show up early or you're fired." She walked away to the back of the store. Which I assumed was the way to the storeroom.

I looked at the guy with a dazed expression. He chuckled and shook his head. "Don't ask," he said, but continued anyway, "Sara Arora." He nodded his head towards wherever she left. It was the way he pronounced

Sara that surprised me. Maybe I held a stereotype for foreigners too, because I half-expected him to pronounce it as *Say-ra*.

"She's a…well, to say the least, a brat to strangers. You gotta work deadset hard to actually get her to notice your presence. Though, literally, we're the only workers here. You and me, now. Do you know what's funny? Her dad collects cars as a hobby. He's a 'car collector', in his words. It isn't even his real job!"

Car collector? Like, her father collected cars? Like how people collected stamps or stickers? I had a stamp collection back at home.

"I know!" He smiled watching me react. "I couldn't believe that was a thing until I visited her house. The old man sells a car whenever he feels like it and earns a ton for doing so."

Sara returned from the storeroom as he spoke about her father. "You do not have to go around saying that to every person you meet."

Mart boy chuckled. "I just find it so hilar– *amusing*. I find it amusing," he corrected himself.

Car collector.

The first thing I did when I got home was take out my laptop.

Car collector.

"You do not understand, kind sir! This might sell very well. I'm afraid we do not have the money to build a sculpture yet," the puny man caressed his beard as he followed the man everywhere he went.

"I do not want to sell this car, Mahen. It's special to me. Now scurry away."

"But sir— the money!"

"The money will be managed. I command you to leave."

The man could do nothing but obey. He was walking out of the room until the sir called him back.

"Oi! Take this back to the kitchen," he ordered, holding up his empty glass.

"But sir— you just asked me to leave!"

"Come back."

Mahen took the glass and simply stood there.

"Leave, what are you doing?"

"Sir! You just asked me to come back!"

"You idiot!" Sir Monte was exasperated.

Mahen could only obey his orders.

Chapter 3

I was woken up by loud knocks on my door. They were hurried— like someone was in an emergency.

I didn't even realise that I fell asleep on the desk. The time was exactly 9 in the night. That would've meant I slept for about 3 hours. Whoa, a new record. The most I had slept in the evening was an hour and a half. Nothing more than that. My parents wouldn't let me, so that evening felt new…. and I felt groggy. Note to myself: do not sleep in the evenings.

I was met by Mrs Jones when I opened the door. She had a smile that disappeared when she saw me. Did I look that much of a mess? Because Mrs Jones looked horrified.

"You aren't ready for the party yet?"

Right, the party! I knew I was forgetting something. I had promised her I would be ready by the time she came to pick me up. I wasn't. When I asked my neighbour to sit down while I got ready, I saw myself in the mirror. My hair was everywhere and my eyes had bags. A very good second appearance I had shown Mrs. Liza Jones.

"Is every place here very far, Mrs Jones?" I asked her as I got in her car. I recalled the mart boy and Sara reacting to me walking for barely half an hour.

"Oh, dear, call me Liza. It's not far, but you don't see many people walking unless it's in the same street," she explained, her eyes on the road. "Everyone living in this small town has a car."

She would have sensed my expression because she laughed when I didn't respond to her.

"No, we aren't all rich. We're normal people who got cars for cheap rates. All work of Sam Arora."

We arrived at the place in what seemed like fifteen minutes. It was packed with lively people. I opened the door and was dragged away quite immediately by two girls wearing the same red gown. I looked back at Liza to see her gesturing me to go with them.

The girls took me to the centre of the stage and everyone got quiet. It freaked me out. Why was I put in the spotlight? How did the people even know me? And the girls?

I saw Liza among the crowd. Philip Thomas was talking to a couple of men of his age but stopped when he saw me. He gave me a big smile. I recognized the mart boy. Sara Arora was nowhere to be seen.

My attention was diverted when I heard the clink of a glass. The same man who had sold me my house stood firm and elegantly. He wore an expensive green suit. I finally spotted Sara next to him– uninterested as ever.

The girl on my right side placed a tiara on me and the girl on the left a badge on my chest. Cheers erupted through the audience as they clinked their own glasses and drank.

The girls that were holding onto my arms let go, smiled at me and walked away. I stood alone there, processing everything and looking like a fool.

"Hey. Newbie. Having a good time?" Mart boy got to me an hour later. I was sitting on the corner of the couch, next to the old men who bickered about the things people did at the party.

"Don't, they hate that," I told mart boy, pointing at the men when he was just about to sit on the arm of the couch.

Mart boy looked amused. He sat on the table that was next to the couch instead. "So, I guess you've already made friends?" He eyed the old men.

I turned my head and was greeted by Tom, Greg and Philip.

I shrugged and shook my head. "Don't say friends out loud. They like to say comrades."

He nodded slowly before grabbing onto my arm. "Okay, let's get out of here."

"What—"

We were in the corner of the huge hall before I could even complain.

We ran into two people my age. One of the two I knew. Sara.

"Newbie!" The other boy laughed. Only then did I realise, that was what was written on my badge, 'Newbie'. How embarrassing.

"Meet Oliver, and you know Sara. Oh, I'm Aaron," Mart boy introduced.

"Nice to meet you. I'm Barkha," I smiled at the three. Sara didn't reciprocate the smile.

"Don't get too hung up at this party, I need you for work tomorrow," Sara said.

I nodded "Yes, boss," to which the boys snickered.

"Boss," they imitated.

"Shut up," Sara replied.

"Let's dance!' Oliver exclaimed and ran to the floor. He was not a good dancer, but he made up for it by making all of us laugh at his moves.

The night was long, with us dancing almost the entire time. I couldn't regret coming to the party. I wouldn't have seen Philip Thomas close to breaking his spine when he tried to dance. The poor man had to be taken to the doctor who was also at the party and was restricted from moving the whole night. His friends nagged at him while he blocked his ears. "I told you not to throw your walking stick away!"

Living in this town was going to be fun, I thought.

Chapter 4

"Sam Arora??"

"Sam Arora." Liza Jones grinned as I threw my head back on the car seat.

Why couldn't I have just connected the dots? Sam Arora, Sara *Arora*. Sara 'I'll lend you one of my father's cars' Arora. Sam 'You're new to the town so let's make a big deal about it' Arora. I found it out when Liza told me. No wonder Sara stood beside him when I was welcomed grandly.

Sam was some man. Liza told me he did the 'welcoming ceremony' for every new person in town. She also told me he managed the real estate and had invested in every shop. Every single shop there.

"So why do they need to give out cars?" I asked her.

"I don't know. They're really nice people. Employees at the cafes and marts he owns get free cars, how cool is that?"

When she stopped the car in front of her house, I noticed a navy blue car parked near my house.

"A Birchfield, darling, you're lucky. That's a limited edition," Liza said matter-of-factly.

"I feel…lucky."

We bid our goodbyes and she left me standing, staring at the car.

At my doorstep was a pink envelope and on it, golden letters that spelt out my name. It made me feel important.

Inside was a Birchfield key to a Birchfield car. Birchfield sounded sophisticated; like a luxurious Ivy League school.

I almost missed the note that slipped out when I opened my front door.

'Arrive by 9 am Do not be late,' it said.

So, there I was, the next day, staring at the Birchfield. Again.

The sound of an untuned guitar made its way to…I was pretty sure the ears of the whole town. A boy sat on the porch steps of a house. His hair was parted to one side. His eyes piercing blue, and black at the same time- because of the heavy makeup he wore around those eyes. His lower lip had a lip ring (I was betting on my life that was fake) and he wore all black. He was what everyone would ideally describe as *emo*. I tried so hard not to burst out laughing when he looked up at me with his electric eyes. I hoped it was all just a phase for him. He looked about thirteen, still young. I went back to staring at the car since his gaze was starting to become a little intimidating, which was embarrassing for me– why would a tiny teenager be scary?

I remembered being so glad it wasn't the States because then I'd have to sit in the passenger's seat to drive. *Number one*, I made a mental note. The first similarity I found between Australia and India.

No, that time I was staring at it because I could clearly see it under light. The car was full of neon pink sticky notes folded in half and stuck everywhere. My name, in gold, on the folded parts.

The first note I opened was on the steering wheel. '*Handle with care*', it read. So did the ones on each other part of the car. Sara was something else.

The last of the notes was stuck on the radio. It had the same message— Handle with care. Only it had a smaller message on the bottom, 'The radio only has one station. Deal with it'.

With a sigh, I started the old car. I never in my life would have thought I would enjoy a strong breeze. Driving in the convertible felt so relaxing that I forgot to stop at the convenience store. Or rather, I drove past it on purpose. Just to enjoy the drive more. I took the car to places it might have not even seen. *I* never saw these places, of course. There were two ethereal green lakes on my way to nowhere. The houses and stores looked old-fashioned. Vintage, like the Birchfield. I wondered how old the town was. Sam Arora was all I knew about the place. How he ran it, how he was the richest— possibly even outside the small town. Liza had told me he was nice; that they all were. But by the tiny interactions I had with Sara, I wasn't sure about that. Mart boy *had* mentioned she wasn't nice to strangers. I felt like I was already on her wrong side, and I had to make it right in time. I *would*, right? Because what really mattered was the unfinished book. What mattered was I had to have enough money to survive. A mart job was not going to get me side-tracked from what I really came here for. Hoping I'd sell a bestseller was still *hoping*. By the pace I was writing in, it would remain *hoping*. I wanted to make it happen.

I had to get Sara to notice me. Then she could (might?) help me with the book. She should know the town as well as her father.

I figured arriving late was the last thing that would get her to like me… when I saw the time on my watch. I was leaning on the car, having no clue as to where I was, or how to get back to any place I knew. I didn't *know* any place but my house and the store. I *knew* I was pretty far away from both of those. Well, goodbye world.

Chapter 5

I somehow made my way back to the mart. I made eye contact with the same guy who was selling damper breads the previous day. I sat in the car and we observed each other for moments. As quick and sly as a fox, I unfastened my seat belt and ran to the doors of the store. The man watched me and tried catching up with me just as quickly. I was a centimetre away from him as the doors closed between us. I passed him an evil smirk when he dropped his hands in disappointment. No dampers today as well. I was successful.

When my body turned 180 degrees, it turned back immediately, facing the closed doors again. Behind me was an eviler person I was too much of a coward to face. "You," she said. Was one word enough to build goosebumps on my body?

"Oh man," a boy's voice exclaimed. "I was hoping newbie would stay for long—"

He was cut off by a 'shush' by someone else.

"Mind explaining why you're late on your first day?" Sara ignored the boys.

I cringed and faced her slowly. The only option I had was to lie. "I lost my way—"

"What!" her voice cracked from how surprised she was. She cleared her throat and asked, "How could you miss it?"

When she saw my face masked with confusion, she snatched the car's key from my hand. Sara swiftly opened the cylinder-like keychain and out fell a rolled-up piece of paper. She unrolled it and held it in front of my face. A map, from my house to the store. I gaped at her.

"I'm sorry, but how would I…" I stopped talking. I was at a loss for words.

"Did you not read the notes I left in the car?"

"I did, but I read nothing but 'Handle with care'," I pointed out.

She sighed exasperatedly, her expression screaming, 'I have to deal with you for a long time and you're already annoying me'. "And I'm betting you didn't check under the driver's seat? Of course you didn't." She raised her hands in the air and walked away. "What was I thinking, hiring you?" she mumbled as she went.

I turned my head to the two boys in disbelief. One of them– Oliver, I recalled– chuckled. "Welcome to Sara Arora's life." He checked his watch, "Oh, man! I'm late again. See ya, newbie! Bye, Aaron."

I watched as Sara rushed out of the mart a few seconds later too, packing books into her bag on the way. I noticed the damper bread man about to approach Sara, but didn't, seeing her face. He must have recognised her, how lucky.

"What does she do?" I asked Mart boy.

"Who, Sara?"

"No, the woman walking past the street now," I replied.

"How do you expect me to know that?" He asked but shut up when he realised I didn't actually mean what I said. "Sara works as a fashion designer," he answered anyway, "Surprising, right? She looks like the businesswoman type."

"Also…are you sure Sara isn't like this usually?"

"She spoke about firing you if you were late yesterday, didn't she? Why do you think she didn't fire you? She likes you." Aaron smirked.

"I'm very flattered."

"You should be, really. Wait for a few days and she'll behave human with you."

I stretched, yawning as I billed the 20th person in an hour. "Doesn't this bore you?"

Aaron nodded. "Of course it does, You think I have a passion to bill customers?" He smiled sweetly at the customer he was billing, contrary to his words. "Have a good day, ma'am!" He shouted after her.

"So…what do you actually like to do?"

"I cook. Not as a job," he sighed.

"You know, the way you said it, you seem like you *want* to make a career out of it," I observed. "Do you not?"

He looked at me. "I…never really thought about it much. Or ever. How far can I go with this passion? Might as well just work around wherever I can to earn a living."

I was about to comment, but I was interrupted by him. "–anyway. Enough about me. What do you do?"

"I write. I plan to publish a book in a few months." Aaron did not question the reason for my arrival in that town specifically. I was thankful to him for that.

The silence was too awkward for me not to break it. "What does Oliver do, then?"

Aaron looked up at me from his phone and laughed. "Are you going to interview each one of us?" He asked. Was this not what people asked in Australia as a way to get to know each other? We asked people this in India all the time. When we visited a friend's house, when we attended a marriage and when we had guests at home. Friends' parents, family members, relatives and even neighbours– they all asked the same question: "*Toh kya karti ho, beti?*"

"Oliver is a model. Don't you see, from the way he walks? His body language screams model," Aaron said. He was right. Oliver looked too much like a model. Even if he wasn't one, people would suggest him to be one. Aaron continued, "You know, that's how he gets along well with Sara, although we've all been friends from childhood. She's a fashion designer, and he's a model. He is the ambassador of the fashion company that she works at."

We were both exhausted by the end of the day. Aaron had sworn Sara would drop by. He raised my expectations when he told me how she often bought him dinner, or even cooked for him sometimes. Sara Arora wouldn't do that for me on the first day, but hey, it was worth looking forward to. I returned home with a big container of instant ramen that I could make at the mall itself, with the microwave and water present there.

Chapter 6

*T*he man stood in front of his own statue, shoulders up and wide in pride. Mahen watched as he caressed his non-existent beard.

"Hmm. Yes," Sir Monte mumbled.

"Sir? You like it, sir?" Mahen asked eagerly.

"Like it? I love it! Who sculpted this beautiful piece?"

"Sir, I did, sir! I did!"

Sir Monte sighed contentedly. "Very good. I will give you a huge prize for this. A prize that cannot be matched by anyone of your class."

Mahen's ears alerted when he heard the word "prize".

"What prize? What prize, sir?"

One particular midnight, my thoughts were interrupted by a loud bang, followed by screams. What was happening in the town?

I rushed outside as quickly as I could. A crowd was already gathered around something or someone. Some of them cleared the way to let me in the front. The first person I saw was the boy with the guitar from the morning of my second day there– lying on the ground at that moment. He clearly looked like he was in pain. Why was everyone watching him and not helping him? Why did they have smiles on their faces?

A screeching voice filled my ears. "Gertrude! Oh, dear Gertrude!"

Was Gertrude his real name? Oh, how terrible. Gertrude was meant to be a female name. Hamlet's mother was called Gertrude!

I noticed that the guitar boy had cleaned himself up– slicked his hair back with excess gel, his electric blue eyes not so electric anymore. The eyeliner was taken off too. He looked the complete opposite– less intimidating and much more childlike and innocent.

Just as I was about to ask the person next to me what was happening, he groaned in pain again. "Go, Lartha. Run away from here while you can." His arm was on his eyes, and that was when I realised that they were acting.

"NO!" Lartha screamed. "No, I will not leave you. Ever. If you die, I die."

"Lartha. Lartha, Lartha. You never understand, do you? Never listen to your husband's words. You could have run away as far as you liked and I would let you be. Oh well, your loss," a third person entered the scene.

"NO!" and then another person. Suddenly, the threatening man falls to his knees. The last person who had entered held a gun in her hand.

Lartha looked longingly at the girl with the gun. "Thank you, Lance."

Lance smiled at her and held her hand. "Let's run away," she said. And they do exactly that. Heavy metal music started to play, and we were all just staring at two boys– one dying, one dead.

The crowd started to hoot and clap at the play. Oliver emerged from the crowd with a mic in his hand. "Okayyy, we're all pretty sure little Gertrude wrote the script, aren't we?" He laughed at the boy who walked away with a sense of pride. "Now for the next play– Sadie and the girls!"

I started walking away from the crowd when I ran into Liza. "Weird town, huh?" she grinned at me.

"Why are they keeping plays at *12* at night?" I asked her. Everyone present looked used to it.

"Tonight's the Midsummer Night's Dream day."

"Like the play? Shakespeare?"

Liza's smile only widened. "No. I mean yes, they took the name from there but we're celebrating Midsummer Eve by watching and acting in plays. It's a tradition here, we do it every year."

Later, I found out that Midsummer was a festival to celebrate the arrival of summer. Kind of like *Baisakhi* or *Sankrathi*, but for seasons. It was celebrated in Sweden and other parts of Europe in June, but since the seasons differed so much in Australia, it took place in December.

I walked around with my neighbour for a while. Liza wouldn't tell me when I asked her what was going to happen the next day. "It's best if you see for yourself," she winked.

I told her about how late I was today and Sara's abnormal chit placings. Liza just laughed it off– like she was used to her. "Of course, that's Shay for you."

"Shay?" I asked.

"She used to call herself that as a kid. She couldn't pronounce 'Sara'. Cute one, that is. She grew a lot."

I was woken up the next day by loud horns. What, traffic existed in a small street like this? I looked out my window and oh, was I surprised. I was met with huge hats. Mr Thomas stood at the front, leading the rest of the band. The band held trumpets and drums.

I rushed out one hour later, excited for the festival. Back home, festivals were a huge deal. Our layout went all out, just like the town. We celebrated Diwali very grandly. I was always with Avi, my friend back home.

I watched a group perform folk Swedish songs. People walked past, many holding flower bouquets in their hands. A group of teenagers stood to capture a picture inside a flowery frame. I noticed a few men from the band pass by too. A woman held her baby by its hand and made it dance to the songs. The sun shone brighter than ever. I hoped the start of summer would bring joy and hope to me too, like it got the people of the town.

Mr Thomas came on stage a while later, clearing his throat. "Here it goes again," a voice laughed beside me. Mart boy and Sara Arora both held baskets of popcorn. Mart boy offered me some without looking at me.

"40 years ago, this town was established," Philip Thomas started. "Most of us have Swedish roots. Midsummer is a celebration, it's the start of the summer season. We Swedish people love to celebrate it, don't we? We were at this very spot 40 years ago, with insufficient money to celebrate this grandly. Look where we've come! It's all your efforts–"

"No, Sam Arora just happened to live here," Aaron mumbled as Philip continued to speak. Sara rolled her eyes playfully. "Don't be bitter, Aaron. Maybe if you worked as hard as my dad did when he was your age…"

"Haha, funny. I'd die working that hard."

"Who's dying?" Oliver swung his arms around the two and stole a few popcorns from my hand.

"If it isn't the celebrity himself," Sara smiled.

"You know, Oliver was asked to model for a pretty famous milk company here," Aaron explained to me. My eyes widened.

"Really? Sir, autograph!" I held out my hand. He slapped it away.

"Thank you. I was hoping Cheetos would accept my application, though. How cool would it be modeling with a tiger?" His eyes shone as bright as the Sun.

"I don't think he understands the tiger isn't a real one," Aaron whispered to me.

"Forget that," Oliver sighed, "We grab lunch right now, what say?"

A kid barged on the stage, followed by a group of other kids. Philip's face visibly hardened. "Children!" he shouted.

Oliver took out a huge chocolate from his pocket. "I wanted this for myself. Who wants this?" He asked loud enough for all the kids to hear him.

"Me! Me! ME!" They squeaked.

Oliver and Aaron just dragged me into the car for lunch, even though I denied it. Sara drove.

She was taking us away from the celebrations. We drove through the empty road. I started to get suspicious. "You aren't…kidnapping me… are you?" I gasped.

Sara Arora glared at me through the mirror while the others laughed. "Newbie, you wish you were worth a dollar."

I was welcomed with a green land, filled with flowers and trees. I walked further until I reached the end of the land and the start of a beautiful lake. *Wow.* The place was beyond amazing. I would want to go there just to read books the entire day.

I heard shuffling behind me. "I haven't seen you this happy ever," I was shocked to hear Sara's voice. I had never spoken to her one-on-one, even though I had arrived almost half a month ago. I looked behind us to see the boys setting up a tablecloth and picnic baskets.

"Ah, well. I love nature. It heals my soul," I laughed awkwardly, replying to her anyway. "Do you guys come here often? How did you even come across this place?"

Sara took a deep breath in, inhaling all the oxygen she could. She sighed, satisfied. "We come here only on special occasions. Beautiful days, such as today." She professionally ignored my last question.

"Princess Arora! Oh kind soul, won't you help these poor men set this up?" Oliver called out.

"That's spelt AUrora, idiot," Aaron argued.

Sara looked back at me. "You're the only other person we've brought here with us," she said, and I could swear I saw the faintest smile on her face. I felt like a teenager again. Young and alive.

Chapter 7

The drive back was peaceful. We were all tired from the heavy feast we had. Sara had asked the cook(s) at her house to make everything in the world, apparently, because that's how it felt. Eating everything in the world. I was stuffed to my throat. Hard to disagree, the deviled eggs were something else.

"I'm playing songs," Sara said, turning on the radio.

"Yeah, yeah, you play only one channel anyway," Oliver dismissed her, closing his eyes to fall asleep.

I stared at the faraway hills, now golden under the sun's light. The sun was placed right in between two hills, almost as if a kid's drawing had come alive. Aaron snored beside me.

"–by playing one of our songs. No, I did not plan this. But what better song would you want in this weather and time of the day, other than 'Serenity'?" A sweet voice spoke through the radio. All I felt was contentment at that moment, as the song played. Serenity. Peace. Happiness. *Euphony*– defined as something being pleasing to the ear. The music spoke to me. A bundle of emotions crashed against me like waves of the ocean.

The sky was dark by the time we returned. "Oh no, are we late? I hope we aren't late. What if we're late?" Oliver looked stressed. He got out of the car as soon as Sara parked and paced around.

"What are we late for?" I questioned, curious.

The four of us stood staring down at a million trays of cookies. "Is it too less?" Aaron turned to us in worry.

"Yes. We need a thousand more," Sara was sarcastic, but Aaron sighed loudly. He had called Oliver dense before, but maybe he had to look within because it wasn't the first time that he didn't understand the sarcasm.

"I knew it," he replied. "Come on, we don't want to get late."

"Newbie's going to do the entertaining, isn't she?" Oliver's voice dimmed as they walked out together.

Entertaining? I was scared.

"Hey, don't leave me hanging! Tell me where we're going?" I ran after them.

I was in a huge ground, facing about 30 stalls. In front of me was a banner that read "Midsummer Bake Sale– the grande festival".

"Barkha, it's been five minutes. Come here already," Aaron called for me.

"I don't understand," I answered, "It's *grand*, where did the e come from?"

"Okay, miss spell bee."

While Oliver checked the sound system, Sara helped Aaron set up the cookies. I had no idea why every stall had a sound system to begin with. "Done, finally," Oliver exclaimed. His gaze was on the stall next to theirs. "You see that stall there?" He asked me.

"I know I'm not blind, so yes, I do."

"Suzy. Lucas. Hannah. Oh my god, if I could just–"

Sara held him back. "I hate them more than you do," she told him. "Their parents have serious beef with mine. Probably 'cause we're Indian, and they're super racist."

"Why can't you just ask your father to eliminate them somehow?" Oliver groaned.

"I wish I could. Anyway, let's beat them. We're winning this time."

"Of course, now that newbie's here." Oliver placed a hand on my shoulder and walked away along with Sara. Aaron and I were the only ones left.

"How well can you sing?" He asked me out of the blue.

"Huh?"

"Sing? Rap? Dance? Anything?"

"Uhh…no?"

"To none? Oh, man. Oliver's going to be disappointed, let me tell you."

"Ladies and Gentlemen, we welcome you to the biggest bake sale festival, Midsummer Bake Sale!" A man on the stage announced. Oliver and Sara were already next to me, cheering and hooting.

"Let the battle begin!"

Everyone was suddenly moving around– fixing something, grabbing their mics, adjusting their cookies or cupcakes. A rock track started to play next to us. The three in our stall were red from anger.

The guy at the other stall– Lucas, I remembered, growled as if he were a wolf. "Make some noise for Luke and the girls!" He scraped his voice.

"Why does he sound like that?" Oliver was disgusted. "And why are people around their stall? This won't do. Come on Sara, show us what you've got." He went over to the sound system and turned up the volume. The music here was completely different from the rock music in the rival stall. In fact, it was calm and happy. I recognized the song. Sara had played it in the car that afternoon…*Serenity*.

Sara started to sing, leaving everyone mesmerized. People started to stop in front of our stall. Their mouths were wide open. Lucas stopped singing, focusing on her voice the same way the customers did. The leaves on the trees seemed to dance to Sara's melodious voice. How didn't I guess she was a singer? She had a sweet voice when she spoke too. I didn't know if it was her voice or the song itself, but something about it brought me back home.

Home. What was home to me, really? I knew I called the town my home, but was it? Or was home my parents' house? Was I wrong to shift to a different country? Did I make a wrong choice, or did I finally find my real home– *the town*? Was I starting to miss my house back in India? My parents? My layout? The comfort zone I had created for myself and wrapped around me like a big, fluffy blanket? *No*, I told myself at that moment, *I left home for a reason*. The town was my new home, and I was already starting to knit my own blanket there. I don't need the old one anymore…right? Barkha? *Barkha..?*

"Barkha!" Oliver shouted to me, breaking my flow of thought. "Mate, you okay?"

"Yeah. Yes. I'm sorry. What did you say?"

"I said we need something energetic. Sara says she doesn't want to sing anymore," he glared at her.

She shrugged. "What? I sang one song, isn't that enough?"

"Right, and you were the one sure about winning this time. Whatever, Barkha's going to take over."

"What? No? I don't know how to sing!" I wasn't going to embarrass myself in front of people two weeks in. It was embarrassing enough when they showed me off to the entire town, with the tiara and all.

"Come on, newbie! Please? For us! For Aaron? You know he has a great passion for cooking. Won't he be disappointed when you don't end up helping him in this? It's the only way to attract customers here! That's the tradition," he whispered to me.

I exhaled. "...Oliver, I'm really sorry but I'm bad, really bad at singing. I wish I could help you, Aaron. I'm sorry."

The boys sat down together in defeat. It wasn't like they could force me, either. Sara stared at me with a blank face. Then I came to a realisation, a thought, an *idea*. "Are we allowed to dance?" I asked Oliver. My smile got bigger with Oliver mimicking my expression.

His hands quickly worked on the sound system after I whispered to him. Sara looked with confusion. Aaron was busy giving away boxes of cookies to his customers. Bonus points to whoever designed the poster behind the stall. A familiar tune started to play.

"Wait. *Wait*. No way." Sara jumped with shock as I pulled her up and dragged her to the front so we had some space. She felt the same excitement as me.

I started to dance and she followed my steps. How could we, being Indians, not dance to *Chikni Chameli*? How could we, being Indians, not *dance*? Especially to our songs! People started to gather around the stall. and the two of us never stopped dancing. I noticed a girl coming our way. She stood in front of us and gazed for some time before breaking into a dance. One after the other, everyone passing by stopped to dance or watch us. Sara held my hand and turned me around. For the first time, I saw tiny dimples on her cheeks. What was surprising was that Oliver joined us too. The number of people coming to our stall increased; they disappeared from the other stalls– the rival stall included. I was loving it all. *That* was definitely home.

Chapter 8

"Hey, Barkha?"

"Barkha, hey. Hey Barkha? Barkha?"

"What?" I asked Oliver, already sick of him.

"Barkha, you were amazing last night," he replied for the 100th time.

"So I've heard," I smiled. "Well, all thanks to Sara and you. You were both *good*. I only got the idea."

Sara was speaking to someone on the phone and as I said that, turned her body away from me and walked in the other direction. Aaron chuckled. "She cannot take compliments for the life of her."

Oliver, in contrast, had his shoulders up at my words.

"But, really, Barkha, thank you so much. I owe you cookies," Aaron told me. My mouth was sore from the sweetness. Last night I loved the cookies he baked so much, I ate almost all of what was remaining.

I flinched. "Maybe not cookies. For a while. Thank you. They were amazing, though."

He laughed again. "Okay, yes. But I still owe you. Hey, how about I cook for you guys tonight? We could watch movies?" Aaron suggested.

"Uh, you guys carry on. I have plans, sorry. Maybe some other day," I said.

Oliver raised his eyebrows. "Really? Newbie has friends already? It's been two weeks since you came!" He snatched the chips from Aaron's hand and billed it himself. "You're slow," he muttered to him. Aaron mimicked him.

The customer they were billing laughed at the two. Oliver smiled at her. "See, Aaron, this lady wants you to stop being mean to me." The lady laughed again, smacking his shoulder.

"Don't put words into my mouth, Oliver. Poor Aaron," she grabbed her bag and went to the door.

"You look very nice today, Mrs Brown! Have a nice day!" He called after her, who waved him away. The two turned their attention back to me.

"Yeah, having a neighbour like Liza must be nice," Aaron said to me.

Oliver was amazed. "You live next to Liza? No wonder. Where's she taking you today?"

I got in my car during my lunch break— unfolding every chit I missed. I made sure to ask Sara where they were placed so I could actually find them. She was annoyed when she explained each chit's location.

I switched on the GPS on my phone and the radio next. It had only one station, I recalled. The previous night, I had the longest conversation with Liza. It was soon after the sale was over. The two of us had to walk home since none of us brought our cars. I told her about my dream, about how I envisioned my future. The real reason I came here (excluding the parents part). I told her that working at the convenience store wasn't what I came for, and she wasn't surprised. Her face lit with joy when I told her I wanted to publish a book of my own. She told me she had a close friend of hers who was an author and would love for us to meet. I said, "No, *I* would love to meet him".

I turned up the volume and heard the voice again. The calm voice I had heard the previous day in Sara's car. "I woke up today and I realised, I don't want to get up. I don't want to do this anymore. But then I thought about it and realised, who else is going to host my show? It can't be anyone other than me. Who else is going to play songs and get to talk to people on the show? Who else has the opportunity, the privilege to talk to *my* people? Who *else*, if not me? I find this thought very intriguing. There's no one else on this planet, literally, that can do what you do in your own way except you yourself. No one has the same life as you. That is a blessing, guys. We need to appreciate life not once in a while, but every minute, every day. With that note, here's our song– Cinque's newly released song, 'Your voice'." He spoke with such a light tone.

As a calm melody took over the radio, I was lost in my thoughts. Who *else*? If I didn't write my book and get published, no one else would in my place. It wasn't like anyone forced me to do it as well. I could've stayed in India, heeded my parent's summon to become a doctor and lived a good life. If it was my choice, why *was* I struggling with it? This wasn't why I left the house. AV's words left a huge impact on me. So much that I would stop the car right now in the middle of nowhere, pull out my notebook and start writing. I didn't. Instead, I showed up at Mr Brown's house.

I was met with a face I had already seen. "Mrs Brown, right?" I gasped.

She pointed a finger at me. "Weren't you just at the store a while ago? What's the reason for your arrival?"

"Uh, I think Liza–"

"Ah, Liza? Come in," she smiled, opening the door wider. "Amazing moves you had yesterday, by the way. Everyone was talking about you and Sara," she said, offering me a seat on the couch. "Barkha, right?" She sat down herself.

"Yes, ma'am."

"Oh please, call me Amelia. Any friend of Liza's is a friend of mine. My husband will be out in some time, I think. Do you want to look at his library until the two of them show up?"

"Your house has a library?" I would stay here if I could.

Amelia nodded. "With 300 books in them. My husband is crazy for books, you know."

I returned her nod, grabbing a book. 'A Passage to India– E.M Foster' it read.

"Ah, you're interested in non-fiction?" I heard a voice behind me. I faced a middle-aged man who styled a moustache and a beret. He smiled warmly at me. I looked down at the book I held. "Uh– no, not much. I thought this book looked interesting."

"You can have it," he offered. "I have another copy with me. Hello, Barkha. Liza's spoken about you."

"Hello…Mr Brown. I'm glad to meet you. Liza told me about you, too."

"Let's sit and talk. Come," he guided me to the living room.

Liza had already arrived and was speaking to Amelia. She looked at me from her peripheral vision and smiled. "Did you check his library collection? It's amazing, no? My last visit was two weeks after the previous one, and there were 100 new books. One would think he reads for a living."

The three of us were seated while Amelia insisted on preparing tea. "Oh, if you don't mind me asking, what do you do for a living?" Mr Brown asked me. At that moment, I was embarrassed. How would I tell him I work at a supermarket? I did nonetheless, and his reaction was neutral. Of course, he wasn't going to be delighted about the fact that I bill customers, but he wasn't disappointed either. Working in the mart must be a common job here. If my parents found out what I did, (and if I still lived with them) they would kick me out. People here were more open-minded. Then again, *anyone* was considered open-minded in comparison with my parents.

"Barkha?" Liza snapped her fingers in front of my face.

"Yes?" I was startled.

"I asked if you've read any of his books, are you okay?"

"Yes, of course. Sorry. Well…I don't think I have–"

"Oh, this is Jimmy Brown," Liza said nonchalantly.

"Jimmy…Jimmy *Brown*? Like *the* Jimmy Brown? No way…" There was no way I was sitting right in front of one of the best authors ever. Wow.

He simply laughed.

"Sir. I'm a huge fan, really. It's such an honour to get to meet you. You're one of my favourite authors. I love 'Over the meadows', and 'A simple way to be', and–"

He laughed loudly again, this time along with Liza. "See? No one knows who you are until they hear your name," Liza told Jimmy Brown.

"Thank you, *I'm* honoured to be meeting a girl like yourself. How's your book coming along?"

I was at Liza's house later that day– ranting to her about whose house we just came from. "I still can't believe it."

"I hope that gave you enough motivation to continue writing." Liza hands me a plate of cookies. I've heard from Oliver that Liza pretty much owns an unofficial bakery. One which the people from the town would invade, eat all her goods and go away with not payment, but gratitude. "We pay Liza back with anything but money," I remembered Oliver telling me.

I understood why people came to eat her baked goods. I experienced heaven for a moment when I tasted one of her cookies. It was somehow the perfect balance of chocolate, flour, sugar and butter. Chocolate oozed out of the cookie as I took a bite. "Liza, your cookies…" I said in awe.

"I'll have to prepare a new batch," she sighed. "Philip wants it, Amelia wants it, Oliver *begged* for it, Rachel and Henry said they wanted it for good luck. They're the newly married couple down the street."

"You must be famous here," I exclaimed.

She looked up from the newspaper, fixed her reading glasses and smiled at me. "Well, try living here for almost your whole life. Almost all your neighbours' whole lives. I raised half the kids here. Oliver and Aaron included. Sara Arora too, of course." She thought for a while before her face lit in an amused manner, wondering if she should tell me whatever she was hiding.

"You know, I used to work as Sara's nanny. Work, as in, get paid for it. Back when she was just born, her mother needed some help. She couldn't manage the baby and the house both. And we're talking *way* back, when Sam had no money to afford the maids his house has now."

She breathed in deeply as if reliving the past with joy and continued, "I was just about 30 then. Still new to my job as a nanny. Moreover, Sara's mother was very particular about the way I had to handle the baby. I still remember– Left hand on the baby's neck, right hand supporting the back."

I was fascinated. "And then?" I asked. It wasn't the story that was very interesting on its own, it was the way she narrated it– with so much emotion, so much pre thought. It left the audience wanting to hear more, even if there was nothing else to it.

"And then Shay grew up, and they no longer needed me," she shrugged.

I wished I had known Liza as a child. I could listen to her every night. I would ask her to read storybooks to me. Every night.

Chapter 9

I was getting into my car when I saw the boy again. The boy who held a guitar and strummed aimlessly. A cat that was walking past the street hissed and ran away at the sound. I raised my hand up to wave to him. "Beloved Gertrude, hello!" I shouted to him. He looked up at me with shock and scurried inside his house.

That day, Sara was in a good mood. She spoke to me way more than she ever had. It was the dancing to Bollywood songs, mostly, that caused the foundation of our real friendship. She appreciated me, and I appreciated her. I told her often that she was a very good dancer and a singer. I asked her how she could do both, and she laughed with no humour in her voice. "Have a mother who is attached to Indian culture so much that she calls a personal classical music and dance tutor and they start teaching you at the age of six, then you'll find it pretty easy."

Sara was apparently a Kathak-trained dancer and stopped practising the dance form just three years ago because she wanted to explore other dance forms. "My mother was disappointed in me when I told her I wanted to quit for the time being. I prefer contemporary, modern-day dances," she told me, rolling her eyes. Did I appreciate the tone she held toward classical Indian dance? No. Did I encourage her to pretty much call it an 'olden day' dance form? No, but I did enjoy talking to her about it. She was someone I could discuss festivals with– Holi, Diwali, Dussehra. But she knew less. Sara understood Australian culture better.

Sara told me she visited India once, as a child, but remembered nothing from it. She spoke about her mother. About how she never failed to celebrate any festival in Australia and still does after more than twenty years. I invited myself to her house during one of the festivals and she agreed. Oliver and Aaron piped in occasionally during our conversations and told us how much they loved lighting lanterns and bursting crackers during Diwali. "Sara's understating the festival at her house. You should look forward to it this year. Trust me, you'd be more than just surprised," Oliver's eyes sparkled.

Sara scrunched her eyebrows together. "Mate, she lived in India her whole life. Wouldn't you think they're a lot better at celebrating the festivals than us here?"

I chuckled. "You should come to see how my street celebrates it. You guys would love it." I wondered when I could actually take them back to my house. Forget them, when could I myself go back? *Could* I ever go back?

"Mahen, no!" Sir Monte sighed, frustrated. Mahen turned his head to look back at him.

"But sir, won't it be better if we just—"

"She's my people. Don't you dare," Sir Monte rubbed the part on his arm where a thorn had pricked him. The two hid among the bushes with a few others, observing an English lady interact with an Indian sneakily. The lady had handed the Indian what looked like a map. It was obvious the two were plotting something. It had disturbed Mahen more than it had his master.

"But sir, she's talking to a—"

"I don't care. Put the damn gun down," he interrupted a little loudly. He looked over at the two in caution just to make sure they didn't hear them.

Mahen eyed Sir Monte before listening to him. "Sir, your orders will be followed," he said as he dropped the gun from his hand. That created a loud *rustle and startled the lady and the Indian. The two together looked at the bushes, fear visible on their faces. "Quick, run!" The lady dragged the Indian away with her.*

Mahen slowly glanced at his master. Oh, he was angry. Red, in fact. Mahen knew he wouldn't have a good day thereafter and took two steps back. He took one more step, then one more until his foot touched the wall. Then, when he knew he could no longer move back, he escaped through the crowd of people– soldiers, ministers, that were with them. Mahen could hear Sir Monte shout from far away, "Come back, you! You will have to face punishment! Get him, fools!" The soldiers did nothing but stare at the running figure, who lost both his slippers in the process, and wondered if there was a limit to how foolish a person could be. Mahen could certainly cross the limit, they said amongst themselves and ran behind him to catch him. The soldiers never could catch Mahen.

Tired, I switched on my phone. I mulled over it for a while. Quince? Sinx? Sinc? Synk? What was it? I was starting to get impatient, especially when the math equation sinc showed up in the results. No, what *was* it? I had to know. I had even forgotten his name. I couldn't stand the curiosity I held. They said 'Curiosity killed the cat', but I was dying to know. So much so that I wore my slippers, opened my front door and took off, not even bothering to lock it. After I reached a specific point just a few minutes away from home, I realised and regretted not taking my car with me. What was I thinking, running this far to the mart? I was so used to using a car, I forgot what it felt like to walk a short distance like this. A short ten-minute distance felt like an hour to walk or even run. When I saw no Sara in the mart, I was so disappointed. I was about to walk away before explaining to Aaron, but there she came, out of the storeroom she always was in. It made me wonder if she lived there– in the storeroom. For someone with a father as rich as everyone put together in the town.

Sara held an amused look when she saw me panting for air. "Your shift is over–"

"What's their name?" I asked her.

She tilted her head in confusion. "I…don't know what–"

"The band you were listening to on the radio the other day, that boy, what was the band's name?"

Sara smiled widely before giggling. "Cinque. Cinque is the name of the band. The boy is AV, he's a part of the band."

I exhaled. "Thank you. I needed inspiration for my book. Sorry for barging in like that."

She shook her head, still smiling. "It's your place."

"I better get going," I looked at Aaron who leaned against the billing counter. "I ran here."

He nodded. "Yeah, we can see that. Do you want a ride back home?" He asked me.

"Could you?" I pleaded. "Thank you so much."

The car ride was silent until Aaron let out a short laugh. Startled, I turned to look at him.

"What?"

"No…it's just," he laughed again, "I didn't think you'd be the type to obsess over Cinque..at all. You look like you would rather listen to rock, or jazz. Who would have known you would end up having another teenager's music taste?"

"Hey!" I exclaimed.

"I'm right, though, literally every teen here in our town listens to that band. You're not special, Barkha."

I rolled my eyes at him. "I don't care if everyone does listen to them. They're good, and that's all that matters."

"On the bright side," he sighed, "Sara looked very happy when you asked about them. She's a huge fan. A huge...*huge* fan. Y'all can get closer talking about this band. She's disappointed knowing me and Oliver don't like their songs anyway."

That evening, I had their songs on repeat. Some I danced to, some I bobbed my head to. One I even cried to. "Do I really miss them," I asked myself, "Or do I miss being used to that place...and them?" Why did I think about them so much when I was away from them?

There were some good moments I shared with them that I still remembered. I remembered Aayee waking me up sweetly to go to school every morning– at 7:00 sharp. I remembered tagging along with Baba to the grocery store– I stood in the front of the scooter which he rode. Dadu used to pluck *aamlas* from his backyard garden. Oh, how I loved the sour yet sweet taste of those. Dadi was no less, she bought me a rupee candy each time she went out. The way she smiled when she hid the candy behind her back is still so memorable, and so precious to me. And of course, I remembered him. My first friend...no, my *only* friend. Avi. How my parents used to let me go to his house for an hour maximum, just to watch cricket with his family. Just because my parents were great friends with his parents. Why would they let me go to a friend's house otherwise?

I couldn't sit there anymore, or my thoughts would eat me alive. I needed to take a walk. That night, the sky looked exactly like it did on my first night here. Clear sky– the stars were uncountable, literally. That was probably the first time in a while I had seen a sky so clear.

No, of course, the first time had been with Avi. We were eleven, young and so full of life. My father owned a small car back then, something he was quite proud of. Having a car back in the day was rare, and it sure was a big thing to show off. My mother jumped with glee when she saw the car right after my father bought it. "Surprise!" he had shouted, mirroring the same expression. Avi and his family ran to greet the car and my father with flowers. He took us on a long drive– including Avi– all the way to my grandparents on the same day, most likely to show pride in his new car. Oh, I was extremely happy– not only because I got to meet my grandparents but because I got to sit in the passenger's seat for half the journey. My cousins back at my grandparents begged my father at night to drive us to the sea. That's exactly what he did. My grandparents' house was situated in a village. No wonder the sky was perfect. Avi and I settled on the hood of the car while my cousins ate the ice cream my dad had bought with so much love. We counted the stars until we lost count.

I heard a sigh from beside me. No, it wasn't Avi, it was the kid from the house in front. He lay next to me. I was on top of my car, the same car that was given to me by Sara. How in the world did I end up there? I still put up a foolish smile and said, "Greetings, Gertrude."

Chapter 10

He was perfectly normal when I spoke to him. Gertrude. "That isn't my real name, you know," he said to me, stretching his hand in the air. I gasped loudly.

"Really? Who would've known?" I earned a roll of eyes from him.

"Louis, my friends call me Lou." He sat up on the hood of the car.

"Okay, then, *Lou*, consider me your friend," I ruffled the hair on his head. That particular day, he didn't gel it or style it the way he did every other day. His hair– like himself– was *normal,* put down, covering his eyebrows and the top of his eyes. So normal I almost couldn't recognize him.

"What are you doing up here, anyway?" I asked him, getting out of the car. The poor thing was crying from the weight of two people. I held my hand out to him for him to do the same, only to be ignored. I cleared my throat awkwardly as he got down.

"I could ask you the same thing. But anyway, you looked depressed. Plus, you looked like you needed company." I raised my eyebrows in shock.

"Okay, well, I have a lot of questions for you," I told him, exhaling in disbelief. "Starting with why you dress up every day as someone that has gone through every hardship of life there is possible."

He watched me for a couple of seconds before looking down in what seemed like… embarrassment. Nevertheless, he let out a laugh. "So this is what I seem like to strangers…got it."

My confused expression made him explain. "I do not dress up like that every day. Only on Saturdays. You see, I have a show where I'm one of the main leads, and I'll have to dress like this for the sake of my performance. Most people in town know it, but they barely come to watch." He sighed.

"No, but it is almost always a full show. People come from nearby towns. Everyone loves me there," the extreme happiness on his face as he said that made me want to protect him. "But yes, I do *not* dress up like that. I would never imagine looking like that either…*ever*," he stressed.

I giggled. "Okay, and what about the guitar you play every day on your steps–"

"Every *Saturday*," he corrected me. "I was only rehearsing my lines, ma'am. I ran away when you saw me today because it's embarrassing, to look like that."

"Okay, okay, agreed. I will not tease you anymore about your roles, Gertrude." He side-eyed me when I called him that.

We both sat at the park, and I wondered how I ever got to speaking with a teenager, before sharing my troubles as a writer. Louis was not an ordinary teenager though, and that was set in stone. He was way more mature than people my age. Who am I kidding, he was probably way more mature than *me*. He was thirteen. He told me about the other characters he has been in different plays and his immense passion for acting. He made me feel like a teenager again, even though it had hardly been five years since teenagehood passed for me. Louis was a nice boy, I learnt.

Sir Monte clapped in joy as the dancers in red bowed in front of him. He sat on a throne, an idea Mahen thought was quite stupid. Monte was not even a king, and that annoyed Mahen more than he thought it would. 'Sir' Monte had this sudden and alleged 'brilliant' idea of filming a documentary on the wonderful arts of India.

"And I. I will sit on the throne, of course. The future should look up to me as an efficient ruler," he had told Mahen, twisting his tiny moustache with oh so much pride.

"Of course, sir! People will look up at you," Mahen laughed unfunnily. "That's where hell is, anyway."

"Did I hear something?" Sir turned his head toward his servant.

"It's the birds, kind sir. They chirp for you."

"That I know. Now scurry along, we needn't wait any longer."

"Barkhaa…" I found the dragging of his words extremely annoying.

"Oliver, I swear to god–"

"Okay. I apologise. You could be Sara 2.0. You're a lion. Both of you are," he walked two steps backwards. I kept the loaf of bread on the counter and sighed.

"Fine, tell me what you want." I assumed the sweetest smile I put on my face scared him more, so I wiped it away.

"Come to Aaron's today. Apparently, he wants to cook for you so bad."

I looked at a taken-aback Aaron. "I don't remember saying that, but okay. Are you sure it isn't your stomach talking?"

Oliver smiled sheepishly. "Definitely not. Sara wants it too. Right, Sara?"

The girl looked up and nodded aimlessly. She wore her rectangle working glasses on the top of her head, eyebrows scrunched in worry. "What is she up to?" I spoke quietly to the other two to not touch a nerve of hers. The boys shrugged together. "I mean, she's the daughter of *the* biggest businessman in town, she'll have some job or the other. Her father doesn't discriminate when it comes to his daughter," Oliver said.

"*Or* she might be doing her actual job? The one in which she's a fashion designer..." Aaron suggested.

Oliver waved his hand in front of his face, dismissing him. "Nah, mate, I don't think so."

Sara and I sat at Aaron's kitchen counter, snacking on the chips he had a whole stack of. What took me by surprise was Oliver, he helped Aaron cook. I would never have taken Oliver to be the type to cook, much less help.

Sara was still holding the big tablet, paying no attention to anyone. She was so focused, that she barely looked up when Oliver danced around her in an attempt to distract her. I felt like I was talking to a wall when I asked her what she was up to. I peeped into her tablet anyway. Sara was staring at a text message. A *text* was what she was so focused on? She reached out for the packet of chips but I pushed it away before her hands could touch it, making her look up at me. Oliver told me that he admired my courage.

"What are you doing?" I asked her again.

Sara only sighed, letting her whole body melt onto the counter. "My boss is just being unbearable. I design a no-sleeve dress, he says it would look better with the sleeves. I make the changes and he says 'Who asked you to add sleeves?' Like *what* am I supposed to do? He shouts at me if I point out his mistake to him. Look, now he's threatening to fire me if I don't listen to what he says."

Aaron turned around to face us, abandoning the dough of whatever he planned to cook. "Your boss *is* pretty unbearable. How are you still in that company?"

"*Why* are you still in that company? Why don't you join another company?" Oliver improvised.

"Why don't you start your own company?" The second I said that, all three faces were on me.

"You're kidding, right?" Oliver gaped. Aaron let out a small chuckle.

"Barkha, do you know how hard it is even to quit a company? And you're talking about making my own!" Sara threw her hands up in disbelief.

"I honestly don't see what the problem is. You are completely capable of running a company and making it big," I told her.

"I'm sorry, Barkha, if my town isn't as modern as your country. It isn't possible to do that here. Do you even know that I have to travel to another town for this job?"

"It's bold of you to assume India is a modern country. It is, technically, when it comes to technology and industries. But when it comes to people's thoughts…don't even ask."

"So what are you really trying to say?" Aaron questioned.

"I'm saying, Aaron, that *your town* is fully capable of housing a fashion company. Haven't you thought about your town getting the exposure as well? Okay, I'm sure your dad is famous and all, but only inside this town, am I wrong?" I had turned to speak to Sara.

She slowly shook her head, trying to understand what I was saying. "So you're telling me…that I can open my own fashion company? And how are you so sure people would join?"

"There must be a ton of people in this town who would want to become a designer. We'll figure it out together," I smiled at her.

We listened to Cinque for the rest of the night– much to Aaron and Oliver's disdain. After I had successfully gotten Sara away from her depressing texts with her boss, we occupied Aaron's dining hall as our dance floor. Sara and I eventually switched the genre to Bollywood. I realised then that this was something only the two of us could vibe to, here. Sure, everyone else loved our music, but not to the extent we did. Sara did have an accent, she just didn't let that get her away from our roots as Indians.

Sometime later that day, I learnt that she was Punjabi (though, I should've known from her surname *Arora*). She stopped talking to me in her language the second she started, telling me that she was obviously "butchering the beauty of the language".

As for the dough Aaron was making…I was horrified to find out what it turned out to be. *Damper* bread. The same bread that the man sold outside Sara's shop.

Aaron was smiling widely at me, presenting the bread with pride. "Welcome to Australia."

I laughed out loud. "I tried so hard to avoid this, yet it found its way to me."

Upon seeing their confused expressions, I explained to them the way I had been running away from the man that sold them for one month– from the day I came to Australia.

I tried the bread anyway, along with the sour dip that Aaron made all by himself. I had to admit, I absolutely loved the taste of the bread. It felt homely, although we never ate bread in our house. My mother told me that she would rather make *rotis*. I never complained since I didn't have a liking for bread either. Yet, sitting at one dining table together and conversing, without any distractions, felt like home.

Chapter 11

Sara's company was on my mind the whole time I drove back home. '*How are you so sure people would join?*' I wasn't sure, at all. The town was smaller than I thought it was. What was the assurance that many would join? There was no assurance. Plus, with an existing big company consisting of several people in the town, there weren't many left to employ. Sara should do something that could engage with everyone, for maximum participation. Should she just join another company? It would be of no use since she would get into the same cycle I motivated her to get out of. What could she do? She could design dresses, and sell them. A… shop. '*That was it!*' I felt like eureka had hit me. Sara could open a dress shop! Why didn't anyone think of this before I did?

The joy in Sara's voice was satisfying as I immediately called her to share the idea. She never stopped thanking me that night. Well, at least one of us was starting to step on the path of success. Being a writer, I didn't know when I would be done with my book. However, I was proud I made progress. I had started writing the book back in India, though I didn't get much time to write– considering the pressure of the job I had. One month ago, I had about 500 words with me. I reached 2500 later. Mahen, my character, was a real, alive person to me. Was it how every author felt?

I only increased the speed of my writing after meeting Jimmy Brown. He gave me a different kind of motivation altogether. The kind a senior artist would give to a novice. I felt extremely grateful to Liza for it. I needed to give her a visit.

I parked my car right outside her house after I returned from Aaron's and rang the bell. "It's me, Barkha!" I shouted to her when she asked for my identity.

"Come in, sweetheart. The door's unlocked."

I was greeted by the fresh smell of a bakery when I opened the door. I could barely see any furniture. The only thing I could see were cookies–plates of them on the table, sofas, on drawers and where not. Liza wiped her flour hands on her pink apron before greeting me with a familiar, warm smile. "It's been weeks since I've seen you! Busy with your friends?" She asked in a teasing manner.

"It's been one week, aunty. And you were busy, not me. You don't step out of your house!"

Liza held an amused expression. "What?" I asked her.

"Aunty. I like the sound of that. Continue calling me that."

I smiled sheepishly at her. "I'm not used to calling older people by their names. Back in India, it's very unusual," I explained to her.

"That's 'righto. And I did not step out because…well, you see." She gestured around her with her hands.

"You spent a *week* making all of this?"

She giggled. "No, silly. I made all of this today. I had other things to do, y'know. Decorations."

I processed this information and came to a conclusion. Excitedly, I asked her if she was finally opening her official bakery.

She sighed. "Unfortunately, no. I'm just prepping for the biggest person's birthday bash."

"...Jimmy Brown?"

"No," she giggled for the second time, "Sam Arora. His 50th birthday, so he's obviously making a big deal out of it. The whole town is invited. Have you not heard about it from your friends?"

I was taken aback. "They didn't tell me. Uh...when is it?"

"Day after tomorrow. A lot of people from his mother's side are coming. From India!" She gleamed at me, as though I would know them just because they were from the same country as I was.

I had one question only: why did not any of them tell me about Sara's father's party? Was Sara not involved in the preparation? What about Oliver, who was the most excited for any party? Okay, that was three questions.

I confronted Aaron about it the next day at the mart. He was quite surprised that I didn't hear about it in the first place since it was the talk of the town. "Sara did not want to make it a bigger deal than it already is, by talking about it more. Oliver was forbidden to speak about it until it was over."

"But...still. Liza says she has been prepping for the party for one week now, so how haven't I heard about it?"

He shrugged his shoulders with a chuckle. "Beats me. People get information through people, you know. The word *spreads*. The only people you have are us and Liza," he said matter-of-factly. I rolled my eyes.

"Also, Liza is an insider, being Sara's ex-nanny and all. Not to add, a great baker. Of course, she'd know about this before anyone else in town."

"Why can't they let you cook, though? You're a perfectly able cook," I asked Aaron.

"My mother doesn't trust him…or any of my friends," said a third voice. I watched Sara and Oliver enter the mart, Oliver shamelessly grabbing a packet of chips from the entrance and munching without paying for it.

"I think she started to like me! She let me be the host for the programs." He shrugged with a smug expression.

"Yeah, but that's because you always are the host. Literally, in all the events in town. The older people *love* you because you're *so* handsome, you are their perfect little model," Sara mocked him, holding his chin. He either knew it was mockery but ignored it, or he was an oblivious fool, because he replied with "That, I know," his expression getting stronger.

"Really, what's with this town? It's been just a month since I came and there's been like a million celebrations already," I told them.

Aaron laughed. "Welcome to our town."

"No, I could write a blog about this town. That's how interesting it is."

"Go for it, make our town famous," Sara had snatched the packet of chips from Oliver to eat it herself.

The four of us sat on the floor of the store right after Aaron flipped the sign on the door to 'closed'. Since it was a Saturday, we had a lot of customers and were pretty tired, me and Aaron.

"Speaking of which, have you thought about the dress shop yet?" I asked Sara.

She exhaled. "Yeah, I'll quit whenever I'm ready. Trust me, I've already contacted a tailor company to stitch the dresses I design."

Sara was a kind of *nepo* baby. A nepotism baby, since her father was so famous in the town. Any company would hire her, any company would listen to her, and they would certainly help her out during situations like these. Only then would they get into the VIP list of the richest man.

"Where did the two of you return from?"

"I wore a suit that was designed by Sara and modelled for it. God, Sara, I really wish you as a solo person would get as famous as your company. Your designs are *so* loved by other brands. If only your boss didn't take all the credit," Oliver ranted and Aaron nodded to confirm his point.

In the silent atmosphere, I heard a scratching noise. It was so subtle, yet was heard because of how quiet it was between us. I asked the others if they heard it too.

Oliver held the back of his ears to hear what I was hearing.

I gasped, "It's coming from there!" I pointed at the door of the storeroom. "A rat!"

Sara shook her head. "Don't be silly, it can't be a rat. My cat would've eaten it before it got to the door." I gagged at that.

"Wait…you have a cat in your *storeroom?*" Why would Sara keep a cute thing like that forever? Why had I never seen it before?

"Store…room…?" The three of them look rather bewildered.

Sara broke the silence by letting out a flustered laugh. "That's not a storeroom. That's the entrance to my house."

"What!" I shouted. I cleared my throat immediately.

"Yeah, the storeroom is pretty much the shelf at the back," she pointed at a huge shelf with a variety of groceries that stood at the corner of the store, adjacent to the door.

Oliver and Aaron both let out a dramatic gasp at the same time, looking somewhat amused at my reaction. "Wait a minute…" Oliver started.

"...You have never seen what's behind that door!" Aaron completed.

"It's *magical*, believe me when I say that."

"It's a picture from a fairytale."

"You would almost expect *Snow White* to pop out of that place."

"No, Alice! Because that place is certainly a *wonder*land."

"You would not believe a place like that exists!"

The boys continued to chatter for a while, then lowered their voices.

"But…would Sara let you see it yet?" Oliver looked at her expectantly.

"I mean, it's only been a month since she's known you. She has known her other friends for longer and never once called them home herself, they are always invited by her parents," Aaron said. "It only took us about a year to be let in by her…."

Sara had already gotten up and walked to the door. She held the handle and looked at me. "Are you going to come or would you rather listen to these fools for the rest of your life?"

The boys did the gasp again— as if they were from a cartoon show. "No way!"

My smile was wider than anyone else's as I stood up and squeezed Sara's hand. "Thank you," I said, quite softly and calmly, opposite from what I was feeling inside. The feeling of knowing that I was that trustworthy for someone like Sara was much, much greater than my desire to actually see what was behind the door.

She opened the door extremely slowly for the effect, and I wondered if her house was *that* much to look forward to. A fairytale kind of house even for a rich girl was unbelievable.

A white cat, soft and fluffy, jumped into Sara's arms right after she opened the door.

"Hi, cutie!" Sara caressed the fluff ball. Aaron went by her side and did the same, and I met eyes with Oliver.

"Please stay far away from me, thank you," he said to Sara. I let out a laugh, a bit too loudly.

"Are you…scared of cats? These tiny things?"

"No, I'm just not a cat person. Dogs are way better," he shuddered.

"He's scared," Sara whispered to me not so subtly, earning a groan from Oliver.

"What is its name?" I held the cat in my arms. "How is it so clingy?"

"She's Snow, and I want to know why she's clingy too."

I was too focused on the animal to notice my surroundings. There was… nothing. No, really. I looked around a dull grey room, spiderwebs hanging in each corner. A sofa was rusting in front of a television that looked like it hadn't been used for years. Okay, I did see *something*, then, if I included the TV and the sofa. The entire room was empty otherwise.

Oliver made the mistake of placing his hand on the sofa because the room was soon filled with dust. Aaron coughed loudly. "Sara, you have to clean this room. Please," he begged.

"Whatever. Come, let's go," she said. *That* was the fairytale room? I didn't understand if the boys were being sarcastic then. If they were trying to make fun of me. I nodded at her words nonetheless and turned around to go back to the store.

Sara held my hand, preventing me from leaving. I looked at her with scrunched eyebrows only to find out her eyebrows were more scrunched than mine. "What are you doing? I said come." She dragged me by my hand further into the room. That's when I saw it– the set of stairs.

A metal door blocked us at the end of the stairs. "Dude…this is like a room from a movie. What are you, the mafia's daughter, or something?" I laughed at her.

"I know right! It's crazy how she created this suspense of a room before revealing God's masterpiece," Aaron seemed to relate.

Sara scoffed. "The room up there is literally supposed to be a storeroom. What I did is better than a storeroom."

"No, it isn't…" Oliver muttered softly to not get on her nerves.

The sudden, fresh smell of flowers overtook the old smell of the room when she opened the door, making my eyebrows stand up.

"You should come here in the morning someday. The night view is just as good, but you'll be missing out majorly."

They weren't lying. I was welcomed by trees at either side of the door, inclined to each other to sort of create an arch around the door. On them, beautiful fairy lights hung. Upon walking further into the garden I observed the variety of colourful flowers that lay all around the stone footpath I stepped on.

Tiny balls of light lay every 20 meters, giving the complete *fairytale* look. The small footpath spread into a huge field of greens, and the flowers only doubled. I noticed a set of stone stairs leading to a big, beautiful pool. Wooden benches with pretty cushions surrounded the pool. The three of them caught up to me. Unexpectedly, Sara wrapped an arm around my shoulder, her other arm still holding the cat.

"So, what do you think?" She smiled at me.

"It's…beautiful. Have I mentioned I *love* nature?" I turned towards her.

"Only a couple of times."

"Why do you guys not hang out here, instead of the lake?" It was a valid question. Though the lake is really pretty, this garden was something else. I stepped on the bridge above the pool.

"Because we aren't escaping. We're visiting the billabong. This garden is mainly to escape from the real devils– Sara's parents."

Sara slapped his shoulder, letting the cat down. "They aren't that bad. No, we aren't escaping from them, but the big party they always host at home. I *hate* crowds. Plus, there's another thrill of driving to the billabong." I didn't ask them what they meant by a 'billabong'. It probably was Aussie for 'lake', right?

I had made out on the very first day when the three of them stood at the corner of the room during the party that Sara didn't like people or gatherings. I had also made out that Oliver was the complete opposite, he was the life of the party. I wondered how such opposite people could turn into the best and closest of friends. Did opposites really attract? I heard from Liza that the three were friends from a very young age, about nine or so, anyway. It somewhat built pressure inside of me, and the feeling of being left out increased. Although with Oliver's complete extrovert personality and Aaron's constant need to make everyone feel included, I barely felt left out. Liza had told me the previous day that Sara had gotten close to me the fastest, excluding Oliver and Aaron. The fact that she trusted me enough to bring me to her garden, again, gave me confidence that they weren't including me *just* because they felt the need to.

"You said you escape from your house to here? Where does it connect?"

When they nodded to the huge treehouse, I noticed it. It stood tall among the flowers, looking so elegant. Creepers had occupied the sticks of the house. "This…is…wonderful."

"Will you let me escape here on your father's birthday?" I asked with shiny eyes to Sara.

Oliver held his heart. "Ouch, are you saying that the party will be boring tomorrow? Even when *I* am hosting?"

"Are you telling me that my father is boring?" Sara asked.

"No! I didn't mean—" I threw my hands in the air, making them laugh.

I slept very well that night, for it was a big day for the Arora house the next day.

Chapter 12

I hated Sara, so much. I hated the fact that she stood in front of the main door with such a crooked smile on her face. What joy did she get from my suffering? From my embarrassment? I begged her not to introduce me to her mother officially yet, it had only been a month. It felt like I was meeting my fiance's parents, no kidding. She spoke so highly about her mother that it scared me. I asked her, "Why can't you just let us meet naturally? I can come to your house later today for the party, and we'll meet each other anyway," I argued, but it was never her nature to listen.

"Don't be shy," she giggled. How couldn't I be, when Sara had mentioned that her mother did not have a liking for Aaron and Oliver themselves? "You're Indian. You pretty much have a discount to enter the Arora house any day of the week."

She opened the door, surprising me. I half expected a maid to pop out and welcome us in, placing Sara's slippers in the correct position after she removed them, but I was wrong. There were workers in the house for sure, except none paid attention to us entering. All of them ran from one place of the house to another in a hurry. It took me a moment to take in her house, her *huge* house. A chandelier hung from the ceiling. It wasn't a house, it was a mansion, I had concluded.

We walked up the stairs, avoiding collision with everyone. On the first floor was a beautiful lady, she reminded me of my mother. She was the only woman in the house who wore a beautiful blue-green draped saree, big silver jewellery elegantly flowing off her. She was so pretty, she could very well play the role of a mother in a Hindi film. Her Indian accent was so strong that it sounded sweet even when she was scolding the people downstairs to do their jobs properly. "She's a perfectionist," Sara whispered to me. I laughed at that. Isn't every mother one?

She acknowledged our presence after a while of us standing there. "Ma, this is the friend I was talking about. Barkha, my mother," Sara introduced.

Sara's mother immediately engulfed me in a hug, surprising me. She said something in Punjabi that I could understand parts of. I lived in a small *gully* in a part of Mumbai, making me a pure Maharashtrian. "How are you, *beti*?" She asked in Hindi and then dragged me away from Sara. Sara's mother's personality was so comforting, that I never felt awkward with her. I didn't feel shy anymore.

I had asked Sara earlier that day why she asked me to wear a *kurta*. The previous day, when she told me, I told her I did not bring any with me. I came to Australia in such a hurry that I did not pack my Indian dresses. "Don't worry, I have plenty. I'll lend you one."

She lent me a pair of pants and jewellery to go with the kurta. Only after getting to the address Sara had sent did I see her in Indian attire as well. 'Was her mother that strict that she can't meet me when I wear Western clothes?' I thought then.

Turned out, a *puja* was happening in her house, early in the morning. Sara's mother (Poonam Aunty, as I later began to call her) had introduced me to some from her side of the family. Each one of them had hugged me the same way Aunty had to greet me. Sara had disappeared to God knows where. The house was so big, if I went in search of her I'd get lost. When Poonam Aunty and I were the only ones around, I thanked her for making me feel at home. We sat on the stairs which I somehow knew led to Sara's treehouse. Although the door was closed. These steps were secluded from the other part of the house. Leaves stuck out from under the door along with the sunlight.

"I'm sure you miss your family, don't you?" She asked. "Do you call them occasionally? I mean, of course, you would–"

"No," I answered truthfully. Poonam Aunty looked so pure and kind, I could spill all my secrets to her. "I haven't told this to Sara, either." I hadn't told anyone that I ran away from home. I don't know if I was embarrassed about the fact, or if I wanted to keep a good impression of myself, still, with the people of the town. They would judge me. They would call me a bad daughter, all of them. They would think I did something back in India to run away suddenly like this, with no plans. Come to think of it– I really didn't. I took all the difficulty of getting a visa, travelling miles *just* to work at a mart when I could instead stay there, continue my regular job and earn money. Live happily…maybe.

I had quit work months before I left for Australia. My parents did not know that. I lied to them every day, and at that vulnerable moment I was in, I almost felt sorry. Sorry for them and to them, both. Sure, they must have hated me for running away. They must have been so disappointed. On the other hand, they would feel betrayed that I lied to them. That I was trying to run away for *months*. They would feel so embarrassed. What would they tell relatives? What would they tell neighbours? I knew that the *gully* I lived in had aunties and uncles who judged so hard. While I didn't care for my reputation there, my parents did for theirs. I felt as though I was destroying it, crushing it with my bare hands.

Poonam aunty was surprised, to say the least. Who would have expected one to act as if the other was a therapist in the first meeting? I was cursing Sara one hour before I met her mother.

"Do you have…plans of confronting them anytime soon? I know it's still too early to be doing so."

I shrugged. "I don't know if that's a good idea. They hate me. They did before I even left."

Her warm smile felt like a bear hug to me. She tapped my shoulders softly. "You know…Sara's father, I loved him. My father did not agree to us getting married. I did the same as you, only with another person. I ran away from home with my husband. We lived in India for one year before his job transferred here, and well, I left my whole family behind to come here."

Poonam Aunty had gone through the same thing that I had, and the thought of it made me emotional. I wasn't the only one who went through this. I knew I was being sadistic, but knowing that other people had done the same as I did comforted me. "I hated my parents then. I know how hard it is, Barkha. Slowly you start to miss them. Trust me, they miss you right now too, a lot. Once you meet them again and talk it out, all will be well." She squeezed my shoulder and got up. "I have to go look at the preparations. Sorry, I couldn't be with you for longer," she smiled apologetically.

"No, Aunty, It's completely alright," I was startled by how shaky my voice sounded.

"Everything *will* be alright. Don't cry." She wiped a stray tear from my cheek. *Why* was I crying?

I shook the tears off my eyes and smiled at her. "I'm not crying, I'm fine. Thank you for sitting with me." She hugged me tightly once again and left me, in tears…once again.

I did not understand the reason for my tears but that was one of my worst breakdowns ever. I sat alone and cried there for what felt like hours. It was only a few minutes though, before I joined back the rest of the people in the house. I went to the nearest bathroom to recover from the tsunami of a cry I had let out. I came out of the washroom and was suddenly faced by Sara.

"Whoa!" I exclaimed, holding my heart.

"Barkha, here you were! How did you enter this place?"

"Aunty…brought me here," I told her.

She nodded with a sigh. "She had to show you this part before I could, didn't she?" She laughed.

I met Oliver and Aaron in the hall when I was next to Sara and her mother. They both wore kurtas. The pride I felt while looking at them was immense. Oliver raised his eyebrows twice at me, shifting his eyes from me to Aunty.

The two of them walked to us after the prayer was over, both wearing a red *tilak* now, thanks to Sara's relatives. Sam Arora sat at the centre of the hall, surrounded by women who performed *aarti*, on the occasion of his birthday. I observed that Oliver and Aaron were the only foreigners in the house, excluding the workers. Even Liza had not come.

"How?" Oliver screamed at me. "How do you do this? Sara *and* her mother in one month!"

I laughed. "Me and Poonam Aunty already have a connection." It made Oliver feel more miserable.

"How does it feel to be the perfect little daughter?" Oliver cried. His expression faded when he looked at me. I must have been holding a very stiff face, my smile going away. Oliver caught on to the sudden mood switch. "I'm sorry, I didn't mean to trigger you."

I masked a frown. "I didn't get triggered, what are you on about? Come on, let's go eat."

My outfit for the evening completely differed from the one in the morning. I wore a long, black bodycon dress, styled with pretty hanging earrings. Liza waited for me outside with her car, ready to take off. "Looking very beautiful, dear," she gleamed at me when I got in her car.

"Look who's talking, Aunty! Have you aged backwards? You look so young." Her face flushed at that.

The day was just about to begin, at 4 in the evening. The familiar mansion came into sight from 500 meters away. It looked different from the outside, now that it was completely covered by the sun's golden light, its front-yard filled with people. We heard faint music playing from inside the house. It wasn't the type one would dance to, rather it was calm—perfect for that time of the day.

I followed wherever Liza took me inside the house. I was too much of an introvert to remain in a crowd of people I didn't know, and the place held the whole town. We crossed paths with Philip and his friends Tom and Greg. The three men greeted me brightly, all of their English accents strong. "Dear, have you been well?"

I spoke to them for a bit and then realised that Liza had gone. I searched endlessly for my friends and even tried calling them but to no avail. None of them picked up. I bumped into Mrs. Brown and was held back for a conversation with her, which, to be honest, was very fun.

She, being just as big of a reader as her husband Jimmy Brown, recommended a few books for me to read. We spoke about being a writer and I discovered that she also wrote poems once in a while.

Half an hour later, I found my friends returning from someplace. I had got back to Liza. We were at the dining table, distributing her sweet cookies to everybody. Sara came and excused me from Liza. Liza only beamed at Sara and nodded.

"You're very early," I said. "Only took you 30 minutes."

Sara hit her forehead. "Which one of you did I ask to inform Barkha about us leaving?"

Oliver hit his head as well. "Aaron…"

Aaron also hit a forehead, but Oliver's instead of his own. "Don't lie. You said you would tell her."

"And I told Sara's mother to tell her! So my part was done," he complained.

As if Poonam Aunty was a psychic, she appeared when Oliver muttered her name. "Barkha! I've been looking for you everywhere. This is where you were? I was asked to tell you that the kids were going out but I couldn't find you," she explained and walked away in a hurry.

"Where did you guys go, anyway?"

Aaron held up a plastic bag of clothes. "Who wants to go swimming?"

Me and Sara got changed into the swimsuit in her room. Her room was just as I thought it would look, very chic and minimal. Also fully white. The only other colour in the room was green, from the succulents that lay and the creepers that hung from the windows.

I looked into the big mirror beside her bed while I removed my makeup. "You could've told me before, I wouldn't have spent time doing my makeup," I cried to her.

"We'll do it together later when the party starts. It'll be fun," she beamed. "This feels so nice to say! Finally, I have a female friend. I was dying with those two all these years. The only person I could go to for advice on makeup and clothes was my mother."

"But I have to agree," she continued, wearing her hair into a bun, "Oliver is a pretty good fashion advisor, given that he is a model and has experience. The other one is simply hopeless," she chuckled.

The sudden thought of swimming in a pool with so many other strangers occurred to me when we were leaving the room. I asked Sara about it.

"No, silly. This is where the garden comes handy. Privacy!"

The garden, no doubt, was prettier in daylight. The sound of birds chirping from inside the trees filled our ears. The trees looked greener than ever, the flowers blinding me from how beautiful they looked. The pool resembled a lake, so clear. It was so peaceful inside the pool that I almost fell asleep. Sara was so lucky she got to live this life every day.

Sara swam to me then, right when I was thinking about her. "I need you to look at a property in two days. Your opinion is very much needed, I'll tell you when. I'm just letting you know in advance."

I gasped. "Are you looking for a new house for me? That's so sweet Sara, you didn't have to!" I knew that wasn't the case at all, but asking her for a house was worth a try.

"You only wish. I'm searching for property for my shop. You're the one who gave the idea, so you have a say in it too. By the way, I confronted my parents about it and they seemed happy with my choice. My mom knows how exhausted I get working for someone. I know it too, and I honestly don't want to do it anymore. So, thank you. Officially."

I exclaimed softly, holding my heart.

"Don't get too happy about it," Sara muttered and swam away, but I noticed the smile on her face as she did.

Oliver was really the town's favourite boy, I came to that conclusion when I watched him host the programs later on. He received so many cheers when he entered– specifically from people of Liza's age and older. The fact that they loved him so much told me that he did something in order to get the love. Elderly people were hard to please, and I knew that from prior experience. It was only because they had met so many people in their lives. They could make out a good person at first glance.

"I was seven when I first met Sara. She was the most lively kid in town, wasn't she?" Oliver started sarcastically, earning a bunch of laughs from people who knew her and an unfriendly smile from Sara herself. "No, she is nice when you look into her. Except you *reaaallly* have to look into her to figure that out. My mother always brought me to her birthday parties. That's where I met her parents. Her father was *the* most productive human being I knew. I never got to see him here, because he was always working. All the hard work paid off because he's clearly slacking now," he scrunched his eyebrows playfully at Sam Arora. The older man threw a popcorn at Oliver, laughing it off. "I'm kidding. I really look up to you, Sam. I want to be you. You're such a perfect person, with a nice personality too. I admire you a lot, mostly because you raised a daughter like Sara. Like, how does one deal with her? Happy 50th, Sam. Here's to more," he finished, and the people laughed and cheered once again. "Next up, an amazing performance by the beautiful dancers who got to perform at *Sydney*." Sara punched Oliver's stomach when he reached us.

Chapter 13

*N*ature, love, serenity. Peace. Mahen had all he wanted at that moment, as he relaxed on his verandah with his wife– facing the serene farm that was owned by his brother-in-law. He rattled the cup of chai with his wife and fell back into his resting chair. "Finally, this is what I want every–"

Mahen was interrupted by the loud banging on his front door. The maid that worked in his house opened the door, oblivious to what was about to occur. Mahen cursed her for her stupidity. He took a deep breath in, bracing himself before turning around to face the red devil– Sir Monte. He broke down into a cold sweat as he studied the angry expression of his master. "You nincompoop! Upon whose order are you enjoying your siesta? Did I not tell you that you had to work at the factory starting today? You are so whimsically staring into nothing, here."

Although Mahen did not understand any of the big words Sir Monte used, he could make out that he was in trouble. His hand reached out to grab his master's hands as he knelt in front of him. His wife was shocked but she said nothing. Mahen acted like such a man at home, she did not know that he had another side to him too.

"I'm sorry, sir. I made a mistake. Punish me if you will, sir."

Sir Monte looked down at him spitefully for a moment before looking at one of the people he had come along with. He nodded meaningfully to the Indian soldier.

Mahen's head shot up as soon as he heard his wife scream. The soldier was holding an iron rod in his hand. "No! If you have to hit somebody, hit me," shouted his wife.

The soldier and Sir Monte exchanged looks and with the master's shrug of approval, the soldier lifted the rod in the air.

A sudden rage filled Mahen as he held his hand tightly. "Don't you have any shame? Hitting a woman so carelessly." Mahen spoke in their mother tongue, Hindi, with the Indian soldier.

"You are our people. You do not understand the betrayal an Indian feels—"

"Betrayal?" The soldier scoffed. "The only reason I'm alive to date is because they trust me now."

Sir Monte was starting to feel impatient. "What are you fools going on about? You, quickly hit him before I do."

The rage-filled soldier did as he was told. Mahen felt a sharp sting on his back as he fell on his knees once again, this time involuntarily.

"Sir," he cried, holding Sir Monte's feet, "forgive me, I beg of you."

Sir Monte held a neutral expression. He took away his feet before bringing them up to stamp Mahen's fingers.

"Sir!" He wailed. "Please. I will…" Mahen looked around frantically. "My farm!" He tried to catch his breath. "Sir, I will give my farm to you. Please, spare me."

Mahen's wife faced him with shock. "Mahen!"

"Just please don't hurt my wife or me," he ignored his wife.

The truth was that it wasn't his farm, not even a part of it was owned by him. His wife felt cheated. Her little brother owned that farm, and how would she approach him after the farm was given away?

Mahen realised this seconds after he said the sentence. Sir Monte, satisfied, left his house and so did his wife, with an expression completely opposite of the master's.

Nature, love, serenity. Peace. *Mahen had lost it all.*

I got up extremely happy one Saturday, which was unlike me. I had promised Gertrude the day before that I would come watch his play. He was embarrassed but thanked me nonetheless. Bringing the kid joy felt like one of my goals in life. Since I woke up a lot earlier than I usually did, I had plenty of free time on my hands.

While the whole of my two hours were supposed to go in writing, I couldn't think of anything. No matter how hard I tried, the screen was blank. My fingers never moved on the keyboard. Instead, I decided to walk outside— get myself some 'me time', without my car. How far was I willing to go without a car, I didn't know myself. I very well knew that the streets beyond the mart were still a stranger to me, yet a trip to nowhere sounded so good, I was fully convinced and tying my shoelaces.

The wind was strong that day, so much so that I regretted leaving my hair open. I was aware that I had crossed the mart that day. I smiled and waved at Sara and Oliver, who had the day off, from outside. Aaron had gone out of town to attend a wedding and Sara suggested that I take a day off too, to focus on writing and taking rest. Who was I to deny? I told Sara that I would come to the mart to help since they shouldn't be working on their holidays too, but she insisted on not to, telling me that if she sat still she would go insane. Oliver was probably just dragged into it with no say of his. I could never have imagined Sara Arora to be saying this on my first day in the town. She was technically our boss at the mart.

The further I walked, the more the population decreased. *Where was I heading to?*

My feet came to a standstill on the deserted road. I stared at what looked like a cat on the road, from a distance. I got closer to the animal, absentmindedly calling it to me. It turned to look at me and that was when I realised that, no, it wasn't a cat. It wasn't even a wild cat, any type of a cat at all.

Gaze fixed on the thing, I stopped in my tracks. It stared right back at me with its big black eyes, which I swear looked like marbles. I would conclude that it was a rat, but it was much bigger. In fact, it was twice the size of a regular rat. Its fluffy tail brushed against the ground as it shortened the distance between the two of us. The face of the animal got clearer and I was sure it wasn't any I had seen before, ever in my life.

My first instinct was to scream. It didn't budge, it just came closer to me with its puppy eyes. I observed as it stopped to lick its paws. Maybe the animal wasn't as bad as I thought it would be. Maybe it was harmless, and I was overacting. I didn't feel embarrassed anyway, since I was the only *human* on the road.

"Hey, you. What are you?" I called out to it again, this time knowing it definitely wasn't a cat or a dog, or even a rat. "Come here, pup."

I held out my hand to the animal. I've had many regrets in my life, from not socialising as a child to showing my marks in maths in eighth grade to my parents. Only the moment after I held my hand out did I realise that I was about to add another regret to my list because the animal pounced at my finger.

Literally, *pounced* on it. It took my finger into its mouth and bit me with its sharp fangs. I let out a shriek so loud, the birds flew away. So did the animal, far away from me in fear. Seeing how scared the animal was made me feel guilty– even though it was the one that bit me.

I breathed heavily as I got up, watching as it ran. I felt a tap on my shoulder and I jumped, moving away. I turned to face a man who looked of my age, or a bit older. He had his eyebrows furrowed as he watched me with detail. "What…are you doing?" He had an American accent on him.

Still startled, I held my heart with the hand I was bitten. He noticed me cringe as my hand touched my body. He looked at the animal that was still running away. The man's eyes widened as he pointed at it.

"A…A possum!"

"A *what*?"

"Possum," he repeated, turning his attention back to me. "They're found a lot in this place."

I nodded slowly, trying hard to forget the burning pain in my pointer finger. "Are you from this town? How come I haven't bumped into you at any of the parties?" I had known half the faces of the town by then, I just did not make an effort to talk to any of them. However, the man's face wasn't familiar.

He shook his head, gaze still on my finger. "I'm not from here, I'm just crossing the road with my wife." He gestured to a white car behind him, one I hadn't noticed before. Surely enough, a woman was coming out of the car, confused at why her husband wasn't getting back in the car. She had a darker complexion than him— it was almost similar to that of mine, a honey-bronze skin colour.

"Tris, what's wrong?" She had an accent I knew. It sounded very thick, like something I had heard from a TV show.

"A possum bit her," he told her, dragging her to me. "My wife is a doctor. She'll fix it, don't worry."

His wife showed an exaggerated reaction when she rushed back into the car. Meanwhile, the man smiled awkwardly at me.

"What are you doing here, alone?"

"Oh…my house is right–" I looked at the road I came from and sighed. "Never mind, my house isn't near. I walked half an hour's distance, just because I was feeling bored. I needed some adventure in my life."

The woman returned with water and a tube of antibiotic cream. She spoke to me about how I shouldn't be swayed by the cuteness of the animal since cute animals are most likely to be the most dangerous ones.

"Still, you are lucky it was just a possum. If it were a kangaroo…" her voice lowered.

I introduced myself after thanking her for treating me. Isabella, the wife, waved her hands.

"It's my job as a doctor, Barkha. Tell me what else we can do for you."

"Nothing, thank you so much. I should head home now," I told her.

Tristan, the man, walked over to us. "Barkha, let us drop you back home. You look very tired."

I was surprised by their kindness. I knew they weren't kidnappers after Isabella treated me, so I wasn't anyone to say no to their offer. Even so, I felt bad for wasting their time in dropping me.

"No, thank you. I would be interrupting your journey, and I wouldn't want to do that. Thank you again, Isabella." I waved at the two of them and began to walk away.

"Wait!" Isabella exclaimed. "We have a day to waste. The town we just crossed, where you live, looked so pretty. Do you mind showing us around as we drop you?" I had figured out that the accent was Colombian.

My eyes shifted to the phone I held. I had exactly an hour left for Gertrude's performance. "Well…If you have time, would you like to watch a musical with me?"

I quickly changed once we reached my house and walked out my door to the couple. I could practically hear Oliver say, '*Found other friends?*' in my head. What was I to do? The three of my friends were busy and couldn't attend the show. At least I wouldn't be alone.

In the morning, when I saw Louis leaving his house, he was back in his *emo* get-up. His eyes were blue with black surrounding them– resembling a panda. His hair almost dripped with gel as it was pushed to one side of his head. Lou kept looking around while trying to get into the car his mother drove. His hand was on his forehead, covering it to avoid anyone identifying him. When we met eyes, he sighed.

I had asked Louis why he was so embarrassed about how he looked when everybody– or most people– in town knew that he dressed that way for his play.

"It has become a habit, I don't know. I would be laughing at myself too if I was someone else looking at *this*," he had gestured to his body. "Besides, you never know when there will be a new *you*, assuming I always look like this. I let my guard down with you, I'm not willing to repeat the mistake."

I wanted to ruffle his hair then because I found him cute, but I was afraid I would get too much gel on my hands.

Louis had reserved four seats for me, Sara, Oliver and Aaron, anyway, upon my request. I knew he would feel disappointed too when he learnt that my friends didn't show up. Maybe the couple I came across had to happen, like *destiny*.

Isabella told me that her husband made music as well, on our way to the show. "I think we would enjoy this musical."

"Oh? You make music?" I asked Tristan. Isabella sat with me at the back to give me company while Tristan drove the car. "What's your stage name? I have to listen to you."

Tristan looked at me through the rearview mirror for a second and looked back on the road. He did that twice before scratching his nape. "I don't post my music, I just make it. I am a businessman." His eyes switched to his wife's, smiling sweetly at her. Isabella sank back on the seat.

In my first days there, I had very different first impressions of the people here. Some, like Sara, were bad. I later understood what Aaron said on the first day, about her slowly warming up to people over time. I didn't believe him then. Some, like Liza, never changed to me. Liza was sweet on the first day and continued to remain sweet. On Midsummer Eve, I had perceived Louis as an average actor with bad script writing skills. Something about the play looked ridiculous to me.

That day, however, when I watched him perform on stage with a large audience, I was moved. In one hour, I had laughed, cried, gasped, and smiled with Lou. Isabella showed her emotions way more than I did. Someone from behind even handed her a tissue to console her.

Louis was only thirteen, yet the impact he brought to the audience was extraordinary.

He was getting his makeup taken off when Isabella and I went backstage. I crept behind him before holding his head. Big mistake, I had completely forgotten about the hair gel. I subtly and discreetly wiped my hands on the makeup artist's apron before smiling at her. She returned the smile and walked away because Louis was now barefaced.

The boy grinned at me from the mirror. "How did I do?" He asked me. "Where's Sara or your other friends?" He frowned.

"They…couldn't make it," I said sheepishly. "Meet Isabella. I met her on the way and I got her here with me."

"I loved your performance!" Isabella exclaimed, pressing her hands together. Louis shifted his gaze from her to me, finally resting his eyes on me, probably wondering how I could just pick someone from the street.

"Well, I didn't just bring her after running into her, I…It's a long story, I'll explain later. Now, are you hungry? Where's your mother?"

"She went to her job right after she dropped me, she didn't sit to watch me perform either. But I understand. Also, I'm starving. I plan on emptying your wallet today," he beamed at me.

"Yeah, whatever. Come, let's eat." I flicked his forehead.

Isabella laughed. "Count me out. I have to leave now…my husband is waiting outside."

"Okay…But why didn't he come in here?" I asked her. As soon as the show ended, he bid farewell to me and walked out of the hall. Before I could say anything, the lights switched on and he was long gone.

"He had to take a call," Isabella told me. "I was surprised he even agreed to come here to watch, he's so busy all the time."

I felt guilty, suddenly. "You told me you were free for the day, I assumed–"

"No! I'm not blaming you," she interrupted. "You know businessmen… how they get calls even on weekends." She seemed embarrassed. We exchanged numbers and promised to remain in touch.

Louis and I had to take a cab back home again to leave for a restaurant.

"You haven't gone to *any* restaurant since you've come here? Like…at all?" Louis wore his seatbelt as he sat in my Birchfield. He claimed he felt clean after he spent an hour in the shower. I couldn't curse at him either for making me wait, it was his day after all.

I laughed. "It's been a month. No, I haven't gone to any restaurant. My restaurant is the mart. I buy everything from there."

Louis looked at me with disgust. "That's such a disrespect to all the amazing restaurants we have here."

I rolled my eyes at him. "You try living here alone, with barely any money. You'd know."

"Why did you come to this small town, though? You could've easily gone to Melbourne or Sydney, or any of the big cities in Australia."

"I hate cities, they're so noisy. I prefer quiet places to big cities."

Louis' silence after I said that disturbed me. I stopped the car to the side when it reached an intersection and looked at him. "That's a lie," I clarified to him. "Who wouldn't want to go to the cities? Those are places one like me could only dream of living in, for now."

"So why did you come here?"

"Not enough money, kid. I could not afford a flat there. I looked up cheap places in Australia and I found this town. You know, I was almost about to shift to someplace in India itself. Then I found this town and I loved it. The rest is history."

He nodded and turned away to watch two birds fighting for food, which suddenly looked interesting. Louis getting awkward automatically made me awkward too– the car still randomly parked at an intersection. Still, the man with a red cap trying to fit huge bags into his black truck was much more entertaining than watching two birds. I wondered then if he were a robber, or worse, a murderer. Either way, it was better to pretend I didn't see him at all. I would get involved unnecessarily...and it had been just a month. What would my reputation be to the others of the town? I had struggled to maintain my reputation as an all-rounder in school all the time. I didn't want to struggle in the town, either.

I turned on the radio with only one channel. Of course, Cinque started to play, and no one was surprised. Louis pretended to puke when he listened to the song, catching my attention.

"Everyone in my class listens to this band, what's so special about them? I don't like them at all," he complained.

I snorted. "Boo, Aaron Jr."

"Hey, have you heard of this food app? It's going viral. It suggests cuisines to you if you don't know what you want to eat. For example, tell the app that you want something oily, and it'll suggest Chinese *and* show the nearest Chinese restaurants as well. You don't have to do anything!" He shoved his phone into my face.

I scowled at him. "What–"

I was interrupted by a gasp from him. "Don't tell me you haven't heard of it! It's trending on Instagram right now. Then again…with an age like yours, I wouldn't be up to date–"

"Hey!" I cleared my throat. I was going to ask him what the app was called before he hit me with the sentence. Louis more or less calling me 'old' hurt my ego. "I know the app." I didn't, of course. But I wasn't going to let him have his moment. I would've known these trends too, had I not been busy at the mart and writing…right?

Louis laughed. "Yeah, sure."

"Who needs this type of app, anyway?" I had given up on trying to convince him that I wasn't a 'boomer', as he referred to me. "I can decide all this with my mind." I tapped the side of my head.

We ended up needing to use the app. Who can decide what they'll eat for lunch if they're with a picky eater like Louis?

"Too greasy," he said to Chinese.

"Too plain," he said to American.

"Too spicy," he said to Indian, though the Indian food available here would probably be a lot less spicy. I didn't get how many foreigners couldn't handle spice at all.

Avi had told me once that he met a foreigner in India who put *sugar* inside Pani Puri. I wanted to cry.

"Eat my head, no?" I suggested to him.

"Ew, why would I do that? That would make me a cannibal." My sarcasm flew over Louis' head. Like Aaron, like Aaron junior. The similarities were uncanny.

The app was on the verge of giving up on him. '*It's taking longer than expected to fetch the results*', it kept saying. Louis had claimed that it was the speed of the answers it gave that made it so popular. Finally, the app came up with Mexican as our cuisine of the day.

"See!" Louis exclaimed. "I didn't want too greasy, and Mexican isn't. I didn't want plain, and Mexican isn't. I didn't want spicy–"

"Okay, okay. I get it." I had to download this app later. "You could've asked Google the same and it would tell you."

"But the answers are from *people*. This app is completely artificial-intelligence-based."

We ate at the nearest Mexican restaurant shown by the app.

Chapter 14

"Have you heard?" Sara lay on her soft, pink mattress. She failed to maintain her full-white room, the mattress breaking the colour theme. "My mother forced me to put it," she had said, side-eyeing Poonam Aunty. Poonam Aunty clarified to me that her white ones had gone for washing and that she had nothing else. "Don't make me the bad person!" Aunty had laughed.

"Heard what?" I was at her desk, facing the beautiful scenery of her garden. Sara's room was a dream room for anyone who studied. It had no distractions whatsoever, and the *view*. That was the reason I brought my laptop along with me, to write as many words as I could in the room. I leaned back on her chair, staring at her as she scrolled through her phone.

"Cinque is releasing a song soon."

"Really?" I gasped. I had become a full-on fangirl of Cinque. Sara was over the moon. She promised me that she would take me to one of their concerts for sure.

"Which means they'll be on tour!" Sara said like she was reading my mind. "Do you think they'll come here?"

I shook my head. "If they do, they'd go to Melbourne or Sydney."

"Yeah, right," she sighed. I wondered why Sara couldn't get a ticket to the big cities because she could definitely afford it, her father being the richest and all.

"Where have you reached, with your book?" She sprang up from her bed to hover over my laptop. "When will you let me read?"

She had asked me this before too, and I dismissed her. "No, if you read it, I'll lose my interest in this." I couldn't explain it, but when somebody– *anybody*– asked about my progress in writing, I never answered them. The most probable explanation I could give to it was that I was aware that people waited for me and watched my process of writing, which pressured me to write. I never wanted to be pressured into writing, I wanted to write whenever I wanted to. I didn't want it to feel like I was working. Sometimes, I often wished I could go back to being 13– when I used to rush back home after school only to not forget the idea of a story I had in my head, then shut the door to my room and isolate myself for hours until I completed the story and lie to everyone but Avi that I studied during those hours. It wasn't as easy to write a story, being a 24-year-old.

"But I'll give you feedback!" Sara argued.

"I will give it to you as soon as I finish my first draft." When I was so far away from completing my first draft, how could I make new drafts and publish the book fast enough to earn money and survive in a foreign place?

Sara had come up with a plan after listening to my problem. The plan was that I take a day off every week– Saturday, she suggested, since she was free on that day– and spend the whole day on writing. I asked her if it would be alright if she lost an employee on a weekend in a mart, *the* busiest day.

"We survived long enough without you," she told me with an attitude. "Before you came, it was fully managed by Aaron. My father told me to put up a sign to take in new employees. Aaron put it in a place where no one would even look. And then you came along…and well." She smiled at me.

"Yeah, well." I shrugged. I felt so proud of myself when I heard that I was her only friend who was approved and loved by her mother, Poonam Aunty. Oliver and Aaron weren't hated, Aunty had just gotten 'used to their faces', Sara's words.

For the first time after I went away from India, I had a full-fledged home meal (*ghar ka khana*, as we would call it back there). Aunty had insisted that I stay for lunch, and I could never thank her enough for feeding me food solely cooked by her.

It was February, which meant summer was already coming to an end. I had spent almost three months in Australia and had found people I could rely on. Aaron had told me to see this town in Autumn– that it was incredible. "It's different compared to what they show on TV. We have a lot of green trees with the red and orange ones, which makes our town look so colourful."

Oliver, then, had pulled out a flower from the pocket of his flannel shirt. "But I'll miss these beauties," he said, bringing it close to his nose and sniffing it loudly.

Flowers. All Mahen saw were flowers– blue, pink, red, yellow. Every colour filled the big field, contrasting with the colours of his own soul. Mahen had black energy spreading out from the centre of his figure– reaching his own shadow. He so wanted to throw the paper he held into the field and wished no one ever found it. He just couldn't, he realised, each time his fingers loosened on the paper. It was the only remaining item he had of his loved one. All other items had left home along with her. His wife.

Mahen had returned from his job as a servant one night to find the house looted. The only thing that remained was the letter she had written for him. With shaky hands, he had picked it up.

"I am leaving for my mother's house. Forever. Don't come to find me – R."

The words repeated in his head several times. She was his only living family, which was why Mahen was so afraid to lose her.

Over the months, he had learnt to accept Sir Monte as his elder brother. He was annoyingly kind-hearted to Mahen. He no longer worked as a machine at the factory but looked after the manufacturing as a manager. He had asked Sir Monte why he would give a poor man like him, a huge role to fulfill.

"I trust you," Sir Monte said.

Trust. What was trust? Did it mean Sir believed in Mahen's abilities, or was it code for 'I have a plan that will ruin you'? Mahen had turned a blind eye to the latter sentence.

"No," Mahen told his friends over tea. "Sir Monte is different from the others. I fully believe in him."

"A fool, that's who you are," his friends had walked away.

He knew. Mahen knew that it was his master's fault that he had lost everything he had. Still, seeing how Sir Monte was behaving with him, he was left speechless. He told himself that he must learn to forgive and forget. That was what his mother always taught him to do as a child. Whenever he complained to his mother about his friends taking his toy from him, she told him that.

He missed his mother, her sweet words to him as he fell asleep, her soft embrace when he was sad or upset.

I sighed, closing the laptop before drooping on the couch. The couch was old-fashioned and seemed to be used by the previous owner. I had asked Sam Arora's assistant if it would affect my health in any way. He scoffed and waved his hand in front of me. "Aye, ma'am. It's leather. Nothing will happen, mate," he said in a thick Australian accent I could barely understand.

Apart from the fairy lights that hung above the couch, there wasn't much in the house I lived in. I rarely spent my time there, because I was either always at the mart, at Sara's or at Liza's.

Liza's home was decorated incredibly. Hers was the opposite of Sara's house. Minimalism was one word that would not describe Liza's house.

I always thought that her house suited her personality. The purple flowers that bloomed outside of her house were just a trailer to the actual house. Her living room was filled with hangings on the wall– whether it was quotes, pictures or dream catchers made of yarn. Her home, like Sara's, had a lot of plants. Liza's plants were mostly creepers and spider plants. Her windows were covered with pots of plants. She had an awful amount of lanterns instead of tube lights. All of that was fine, but what I didn't get was the random piece of cloth hanging from the ceiling– attached from all four of its corners, like someone could have a picnic in the small space between the cloth and the ceiling. The cloth had a pattern that was quite similar to that of Indian bedsheets, or block-printed kurtas.

I had asked her if she had placed it to cover a hole in the ceiling. She simply laughed. "No, silly," she exaggerated an 'r' sound after her 'no'. "It's an…what do you young people call it? *Aesthetic*. It's for the vibes, y'know?"

I noticed her cushions looked alike to the cloth.

"It's called hippie aesthetic," Oliver said when I reported to him about her. He sipped on his afternoon tea dramatically, crossing his legs on the armchair and lifting his pinky finger to imitate typical British housewives. "Liza isn't even a hippie, I don't know what she's trying to prove."

"I find this very nice looking. Tell that boy to mind his own business," Liza laughed to me, when I reported back to her about Oliver.

While I liked their houses, I didn't want my house to look like Sara's or Liza's. I had always imagined my dream house to be small and cozy, and filled with books. I wanted the number of books Jimmy Brown had, though I was pretty sure I would struggle to read even one– considering how occupied I was.

Chapter 15

To help with the interiors, I had three people with me. One half reliable, the other two purely for entertainment. Sara sounded more excited than me on call when I told her.

"If I weren't a fashion designer, I would be a great interior designer," she claimed and got in when I opened the door for them. Sara immediately scrunched her face after looking around.

"Why haven't you done anything?"

Aaron was already in my kitchen. "Let me make something for you. What do you prefer, dust or fungus?"

I kicked him. "It's not *that* bad, come on."

Oliver, surprisingly, was useful. He brought us a bowl of chips that he got from Liza's.

"So what are we doing?" I told them what I wanted it to look like and Sara had got with her a huge duffle bag of god-knows-what.

"These are things we bought for our house but never displayed them because they didn't suit our aesthetics," she explained to me, unzipping the bag.

"...Books?"

Half the bag was filled with books.

"Yeah, they looked like nice showpieces."

I laughed in disbelief. "You don't know how offended I am." I accepted the books anyway.

Oliver plopped onto my couch. "Yeah, change this, mate." He tapped on the leather. "It's so uncomfortable, how do you even sit here?"

"I don't," I responded, "I sit on the floor."

The three of them cringed harder. Sara began to drag me to the door. I asked her where we were going.

"We're going to buy you some furniture."

"I'm saving money! I don't have much."

Oliver looked at Sara with a sudden turn of his head. "Sara…"

Sara, ignoring Oliver, smiled at me. "You don't have to have money. Come on. I wish I had told you about this earlier."

I understood what she meant when we reached a narrow alley. The chatter coming from Oliver and Aaron behind us was now reduced to hushed whispers. The road got scarier the more the sun was covered by the roofs of buildings. Sara was going to do something illegal.

The four of us entered what looked like a shop. It didn't have a signboard, but the insides were full of kitchenware and wall hangings. "Arch!" Sara shouted out. What kind of a name was *Arch*?

A man scurried to us– not big, but not puny either. He looked of Liza's age. "Barbie," he referred to Sara.

"You owe me," Sara crossed her arms.

He nodded. "What can I get you…and these fools over here?" The man smacked Oliver's neck from behind. Oliver smiled sheepishly, awkward for some reason. The man especially paid attention to Oliver, and so did Oliver to him.

"We need the huge bean bag sofa you showed me last month. Also, the book rack that I loved…" Sara's voice faded as the two of them walked up the stairs to another floor.

I stared at Oliver, who remained in the same position. His eyes refused to look anywhere but the floor, his hands awkwardly clumped together— as if he was going to start singing at his school's annual day. He looked at me only when I nudged him.

"Are you okay?" I whispered to him. He nodded and asked for some air.

I felt Aaron come closer to me as I watched Oliver walk out of the shop. "Don't worry about him," Aaron told me.

Sara had returned to where we stood without the man. "Everything you need will be delivered to you in one hour. Now, come. We have a lot of work to do."

Aaron was hesitant to invite me to his house. "I need to invite you *formally* for lunch, not to collect paint! My mother would be so disappointed in me."

We ended up at his garage anyway, while the other two decided to split to get us food. The sun had set, and it was almost dinner time.

Aaron picked up big cans of paint and compared the colours, looking from one colour to another, then looking at me. "Brown would suit your living room, and olive green would suit your bedroom. Let's take both."

"Again, you really don't have to do this. At least tell me what I owe you!"

"It's my dad's, relax. As long as you buy me a house and a yacht."

"Haha, funny," I said, not really meaning it.

He grinned and turned around. Small hands met his and he picked the person up. "Say hi to Timmy." He was carrying a toddler, who giggled when Aaron pinched his nose. The kid turned to me and studied me with a gaze. I melted right away. I had a lot of love towards children, especially toddlers of one or two years.

I gasped. "Is he your little brother?" I touched the kid's cheeks.

"Yeah," Aaron dropped him with a little more force than I expected.

"Hey–" I began to argue, but he interrupted me with a laugh.

"I have more of these," he ruffled his brother's hair. Little Timmy ran out of the garage. "In different sizes. M, L, XL."

"How many siblings do you have?" I asked with amusement.

"Four," he was placing the paint cans in a bag. I switched off the light in the garage for him when we left it. "I'm the oldest. You're so lucky you're an only child, you would die handling younger siblings."

"You'd die out of loneliness without one, trust me. Having a sibling is a blessing. I've always wanted to have one."

He lifted his arms in defence. "Fine, fine. I admit the little ones aren't that bad of a company."

Sara and I stared at each other an hour after Aaron and I had returned from his house. Her gaze was so strong, I felt like I had travelled back to my second day in the town…when I arrived late to my first day as a mart employee.

She was so intimidating, she always made me want to apologize to her for no reason. So that was exactly what I did that day too. She smacked her forehead to her palm.

"No…I just don't understand!" Her exasperated look made her resemble Hermione Granger. "How can you be so blind?"

Sara was pissed at me for not noticing the terrace that was attached to the house I lived in. She lived in a mansion, yet a small thing like a terrace interested her. It was compelling.

"Of course I've seen it," I said, placing pizza boxes on a table we found on the terrace. "I just wasn't that excited about it."

She threw her hands up, the exasperation increasing. "The terrace is *the* best part about a house! Would you not want to hang out here?"

She was right, I realised. The terrace was quite spacious. Since the town wasn't polluted, we could see the uncountable stars at night. It was still evening when we went up so the only thing we could see was a gradient sky of blue and orange. It was beautiful. A short table lay on the edge of the terrace, and a few chairs were clumped together.

"You know what, let's sleep here tonight," Sara told us, stuffing the slice of pizza in her mouth.

"Yeah, we'll be good meals for mosquitoes."

Sara had found the perfect couch for me, even I was surprised. It looked like a rectangular cloud. It had no legs so the couch was pretty low. It felt like a softer version of a bean bag when I tried sitting on it. A truck had come to deliver everything Sara had ordered. The fact that the truck was black made it more suspicious. Was I supposed to simply accept whatever she gave me without questioning her or paying for it? I confronted her when she walked back to the truck to take smaller items. She looked at herself through the fancy oval mirror she held.

"What?" She laughed so hard, she had to hold her stomach.

"What?" I asked back, offended that she was laughing for no reason at all.

"You thought I was..." her own laugh stopped her from speaking. "You thought I was a *fence*?"

"I did *not* say that! I just thought..."

"God, Barkha. You're so unintentionally funny sometimes. No, I'm not performing any sort of illegal activity. Neither do you have to pay me anything, the man truly owed me. He knows my father personally, and—"

"Get this thing out of here!" The sudden shriek made both of us flinch. The source of the sound was Oliver from inside my house.

We rushed inside to find him standing on top of the old couch, making the poor thing dirty before I gave it away. Aaron was pointing his phone camera at him, chuckling.

Both of them were looking at something on the ground. I went further inside only to be pleasantly surprised when I found out what it was. Sara followed after me and gasped, holding her hands to her mouth in shock.

On the floor was a kitten the size of a baby's hand. It had a black spot on its white fur, making it look cute. "Hi baby," Sara stretched her words while she went to grab it. She moved it closer to Oliver. He shrieked once again, running from where he stood to the kitchen. He held the newly bought fry pan in front of him in defence. "Don't you dare," he muttered.

"I told you," Sara held out the kitten to me, and I accepted it without a thought. "He's *terrified*."

I snuggled it close to my heart. "It's so small! When did it even get in?"

Oliver let out a scoff. "When you idiots decided to leave the door unlocked."

Though the same colour, it looked nothing like Sara's cat. Her cat looked elegant, with its bright blue eyes and long eyelashes. One pink collar and a bowtie for her long fur would turn her into Marie from The Aristocats. The kitten I held looked like a white version of Felix the cat. It (he, I later found out his gender) had eyes half the size of its head. It was absolutely adorable.

"What do we do with this now?"

Chapter 16

I knew that its mother was somewhere around. A kitten couldn't be abandoned that early by his or her mother, in most cases. What was the kitten, if abandoned, to do in a street alone? But again, I didn't want to take the kid away from its mother. I would be too cruel. So, to keep or not to keep?

I received mixed reactions from my friends. Sara said she would cry if I let it go. She told me that she would take it if I didn't. "Don't let the kitten feel lonely in my house. Take it. Give it to Liza when you aren't home."

Oliver promised to never visit my house again if I kept it. "I dare you to bring it anywhere near me, I will unfriend you." I wasn't phased by his childish behaviour.

Aaron didn't care. "Keep it in Sara's house or yours, or on the street. I will visit it anyway. I will give it food." He shook his head vigorously when I asked if he could keep it in his house instead. "You won't find it alive the next day in a house of four maniacs."

Sara and I cringed at that. "Oh my god Aaron, shut up." I tried to hold the kitten closer to me than it already was. Oliver was still in the kitchen with the pan. One would take him to be Rapunzel if he had longer hair. His blond hair and feminine eyes suited perfectly for the role. Why did no one recruit him for acting? Based on the way he behaved seeing a tiny kitten, his acting skills weren't half bad.

I took the kitten outside with me first, hoping I would find its mother. I let it drop to the ground. The kitten, which I had expected to run away, climbed onto my foot instead. It meowed for a little while before it hissed and ran back to my house. I faced a much bigger cat. It was a cat I had seen around Lou's house pretty often. The cat hissed back ten times stronger than the poor kitten, that had hidden itself under the couch.

"Hey, stop!" I shouted at the cat as though it would actually listen to me and run away. It did the opposite, the cat inched closer towards me. "Stay away!" I shouted again. Oliver had heard me and cried out loud.

"What is happening outside?" He called out. I imagined how scared he would have been if I was scared myself. There was no reason not to be scared, the cat was the opposite of flattering. His sharp teeth shone as he snarled at me. His fur wasn't dirty, just messy. The cat either wasn't an outdoor cat or was looked after by somebody. I concluded because around the neck of it was a red collar. It had a name tag too, but obviously, out of sheer fear, I didn't bend down to read what it said. My poor eyesight helped a lot in matters like those.

"Snarkles!" A boy came running toward the devil of a cat.

It wasn't just any boy.

"Gertrude, what the heck!" I scolded him. It was one thing to leave your cat unattended, but the fact that he looked after such a cat angered me more, for some reason.

"Snarkles, I searched everywhere! What are you doing here?" The cat seemed to calm down at his presence, melting right into Louis as he carried him.

Moreover, what kind of a name was *Snarkles*? It sounded like he made a spelling mistake and wanted to name it *Sparkles* instead. Okay, agreed. Sparkles wasn't that good of a name either, but it beat Snarkles any day.

He lowered his head to look at his cat and kissed Snarkles' head. Wow, the name was growing on me.

"What did my cat do to you for you to make such a bitter expression?" Louis turned his body away from me, covering his cat's eyes simultaneously. I must have made a very horrified face, for him to be acting that way.

"Tell your cat to stay away from the baby kitten. He's troubling it," I complained.

Aaron and Oliver ran out the second after I said that. "What!" Oliver had noticed the bigger cat. "I came here to escape from *that* thing to face *this*?"

Louis let out a gasp. "Ouch. Hello to you too, Oliver."

Oliver grimaced, still not looking the cat in the eye. "Put that down and we'll talk."

"Sure, if you're okay with it. It will only come to you."

"Should I just run away?" Oliver wailed.

"Shut up. Don't be dramatic. We have a bigger problem here. Who will keep the cat?" I looked around at everyone present.

"Snarkles is mine! Why would any of you keep it?"

Sara, then, arrived from inside the house with the kitten. Talk about perfect timing. "Barkha— keep it. It won't survive long outside."

Dogs were pretty rare in the town. During my three months, I had seen *only* one. That, too, was someone's pet. I never encountered a stray dog. India was filled with dogs and *very* kind ones. I was bitten by three stray dogs at once when I was younger. I got ten injections after. Ideally, the person who got bit was more likely to be traumatized than another who didn't. Avi was a different case. He had witnessed the incident and so, was scared of dogs till the time I watched him leave. Seeing how Oliver acted at that moment reminded me of Avi too much.

The day I watched him leave was the worst day anyone could have in history, or so I thought. We were sixteen, both of us. We had just got done with our board exams. We received our marks, too. My parents were more than proud of me when they saw my marks. 96 per cent, I got. I remembered behaving as though the marks didn't matter much to me. It mattered less to me than it did to my parents, that was for sure. But I felt accomplished as well, I couldn't lie. All my hard work, all the studying for hours and all the nights I stayed up majorly paid off. I was in my worst state then, physically and mentally both. Physically, I had circles as dark as the night under my eyes. I had increasingly put on weight, but my parents didn't care for my physical appearance. They only cared if I got above 90 or not, attended a good college and then worked in a nice, big office as an engineer. Because that was what my father did, too…and his father. They were waiting for the opportunity and time to get me married and sent off. Not at sixteen, obviously. They weren't *that* bad.

The evening I found out my marks, so did Avi. His parents called mine in excitement. 97. Avi had managed to beat me that time. He always was ahead of me, whether it be sports or academics. We once attended a cooking competition with no experience at all, just for the fun of it. He defeated me even there. I was left speechless and gaping at him. The day of the marks, I wasn't surprised. I just hoped the two of us would get into the same college for the next two years.

That was when they dropped another bomb— just like that, on our faces. I was closer to the bomb than my parents were, because I clearly was more affected by it than they were. While theirs were wounds that could be healed in hours, mine was a much deeper one. Avi's father was to shift to the US because of his job…and his son was to follow him there, study and get a great job. I couldn't be happy for him, no matter how much

I tried to be. I was losing the only friend I had made in my whole life. What was I to do without him?

They left the same night. Avi told me that it was his plan from the start. I was angry at him for not telling me earlier. Eight years later and I still couldn't make sense of his reason. He argued that I would stop talking to him if he told me earlier. That was true, I agreed. I would not have been able to talk to him further knowing he would be leaving later anyway. I would simply cut ties with him. Still, I needed to prepare my mind for it. Avi was being ridiculous. I didn't stop him from going. He told me that I always had his number and that I could message him whenever.

I did, everyday after he left. We were in touch for a month before he stopped responding altogether. I somewhat made friends in my new college. I couldn't really call them my friends, *classmates* was a better word to describe our relationship.

"I'll keep him," I told Sara, snapping out of my thoughts.

Chapter 17

If there was anyone happier than Sara about getting a new member into my house, it was Philip. Liza was happy, she even bought the kitten a bowl to eat from.

But Philip's happiness was different. He looked like he reconciled with one of his friends from the army. He doted on the kitten for hours when I had invited both of them the day after I adopted the kitten. Philip was so happy, I was on the verge of giving the kitten to him. He denied. "I would, but I'm allergic." But he had touched it with all his body already. I did not remind him of that. Who would I be to ruin one's happiness?

"What will you name him?" Liza remained calm, she always did.

"I'll name him Liza," I joked.

"Now, don't change his gender," she laughed. "Name him Philip instead."

I was not one to judge a name like Snarkles when the only name I could come up with was Dot. For the black dot on his nose. I was called the most creative kid in my hometown once upon a time. Everyone else, including Oliver, had loved the name, though.

I brought Dot to his first day of work. The work he did? Entertain us while we billed customers. No one was against it. My manager was the most thrilled about it. "How about we turn it into a cat cafe instead?" Sara was hyped. I asked her to start her clothing business first.

"I quit my job," she told us one day, opening the door to the mart hurriedly. Oliver was with her. He maintained a distance from the counter, where Mr. Dot was sleeping.

"You should've seen the look on her boss' face when she gave her resignation letter!" He laughed, nodding.

"Wait, what? Why were you with her…no, forget that. Sara, what!" I was proud of her as though she was my little sister. She hugged all of us tight that night.

I went with her weeks ago to check the property out. Sara had bought a ton of chips from her own mart to suffice us for a year. It was not even that far, yet she took her car on a ride. Typical Arora behaviour. It seemed like it was near the center of the town. I knew this because I recongnized the place from the Midsummer day, when the band had stopped and played for what felt like centuries. Also, where Philip spoke about the heritage of the town.

The shop was quite big, and empty. It had several rooms inside of it.

"Was it originally a clothing store? These look like trial rooms."

"Yeah, it was. It belonged to my dad's friend," she replied. I stopped and held her hand, making her stop with me. She raised her eyebrows at me.

"Don't tell me you made the original owner unemployed with your money…"

Sara laughed. "You read too many novels. No, Barkha. God. He shifted away recently. This shop was *completely* empty. My father might be rich but he's also a good man," she clarified.

I mean, I never got the chance to interact with her father fully. Sam Arora was a busy man. He was rarely at home when I went to visit. I only partially knew him through the stories his wife and daughter told me. I was closer to one of their maids, than him. It was natural of me to judge him. Rich people could be self-centered and greedy sometimes. Bahadur Rao of my gully taught that to me. He was a big don back in the days, and extremely rich.

Sam's mother was a Christian. She wanted her beloved granddaughter to have a Christian name as well, hence the name Sara. I did not ask that to her directly, of course. That would seem rude. I asked her mother instead. Not like it made a huge difference.

I fully approved of the shop we had looked at, though my opinion was as important as a stranger's was. Sara thought otherwise.

"What, were you seriously going to look for another property if I said I didn't like this one?" I asked her.

"No," she admitted. "Your opinion is important nonetheless," she said sheepishly.

"What will you name the shop?"

"Incanto," she exhaled, stretching her hands toward the sign on the shop. "It's Italian for enchantment. Isn't that so beautiful? I can't believe I'm finally opening a shop of my own! I just have to quit my job now."

Sara did, on the day Dot slept. Too bad he couldn't enjoy the little moment the four of us had. Were he awake, he would have supported Sara too.

"Where have you reached?" I wanted to stab her first, and then myself. Not literally. I loved Liza.

I simply hated the question. Where had I reached? Nowhere. I had made no progress. Nothing at all. Zilch.

"I don't know!" I dragged my words. "I'm so annoyed that I can't continue. It's so stressful. No one's even putting the pressure on me," I whined.

Liza gave me a weird look before nodding. "You don't have to feel stressed about redoing your house, you know that, right?"

It occured to me later that she was not talking about the book I was writing.

"Are you okay?" She asked me when I kept quiet. I laid on her couch, staring at the ceiling. I wished I could be the cloth then. It did nothing, it just had to hang and collect dust. How nice its life must have been. How lunatic I must have been, wishing to be a cloth.

"Life is just…not going the way I planned it to be going. Sara is making so much progress. She left her job, she already started to design clothes and hand it over to her tailor from a company. Everything is going in her favour. Whereas I am…what am I doing, in life?"

Liza let out a chuckle she didn't really want to let out. "Sorry," she apologised. "I just found it funny how a young girl like you spoke about… life…I'll stop." I knew she could feel my glare at her.

"I finished painting my house with the three of them," I answered her first question. "Now I just need to organize the clump of furniture. Also, Sara got that illegally?" I loved spreading misinformation.

"What? Sara wouldn't—"

"She got it for free in a suspicious shop, in some corner of somewhere…"

Liza laughed. "That is Arch," she said, as if it helped me so much. This mysterious man was getting on my nerves. I was itching to know who he was and get over with it. If his shop was in the open, I would let it go. Maybe he just liked darkness. Pro tip number one from a professional property chooser: never open a shop where no one can see it or you don't get customers at all. Why would he open a shop if he didn't welcome customers? It beats me.

Mahen stared at the factory. Was he really going to do it? He didn't know it himself. He knew it was wrong— anyone could see that he was hesitating to go inside. He still needed it. He did not know if he was being selfish or greedy.

Or both. He did not care either. At that point, it was the only thing on his mind. The only thing he worried about was if his wife would distance herself further from him. If everyone distanced themselves from him. His friends, his living relatives. His neighbours and the shopkeepers he loved talking to. They might all run away. It was ironic because he was going to do it only to maintain and strengthen the relationships he already had, and get back his wife. Some might praise him, but would he choose to remain with those that would praise him, or would he pursue the ones that ran from him? No one knew. He did not know it himself. Mahen knew nothing. He had one thing and one thing only on his mind. To get rid of everyone. Everyone that dared to lay hands on the people he loved and adored. Everyone he wished would rot in hell. Hell was a horrible place, he had read in a magazine. In hell, the bodies of the people that commit sins burn. The people are forced labourers. If they did not listen, the devil god himself would come and punish them. What kind of a punishment can exist beyond burning bodies? Only the people that were in hell could answer that. Mahen wanted to know, but going to hell himself was the last thing he wanted to do. At that point, Mahen had come to a conclusion. If the people don't go to hell for their unforgivable sins, he would bring hell to them himself. Before the servants of hell did it, he would burn the body of every single person at the factory. That included his beloved Sir Monte. How would he feel after doing it? He did not know himself.

"What are you so focused on, instead of the customers?" Oliver was by my side out of the blue. I jolted away, quickly closing the book I was writing in. Carrying a notebook to work was not a bad idea, I learnt. I couldn't get my laptop to work, so the notebook was perfect for me. I would always get ideas at the most random times. Ideas that would disappear if I didn't write it right away.

"Just...my writing," I stuttered. Why I stuttered, I had no clue. Writing was not something I wanted to hide, ever. I should have been proud that I could work as well as do what I want to.

The book was out of my hands before I knew it. Oliver.

"Oliver. Give it back. I'm not even kidding, I'll get Snarkles to you. Don't read it– Oliver!"

He was sprinting around the mart with my book. I found it very embarrassing to be running around like we were children in front of customers. Especially as workers... no, *a worker* here. Oliver did not care at all.

On the other hand, he would read all of what I wrote. Again, I should not have been hiding it. But I couldn't help it. What I had written was far from readable. I needed to redraft it several million times before someone could get to read it. I was too much of a perfectionist, it was my biggest flaw. I needed constant reminders to relax.

I really missed Aaron. The replacement Sara had found was the opposite of my original co-worker. The dude never spoke. And I meant it, *never*. If I was considered an introvert, that guy was on a different level. He maintained the same expression throughout– as though he was someone's bodyguard. Given his big figure, I wouldn't be surprised if he actually was a former bodyguard. Aaron had escaped work once again, giving the petty excuse that his father needed help with building an I-don't-even-remember-what. Or maybe he was really helping, one wouldn't know. Sara was busy with the designing and stitching of her dresses, and could not make it to the mart. Oliver had just got off work– earlier than he expected to. He bragged to me about how he was done with work after the first picture they clicked of him. Oliver, supposedly, looked too natural that they got over with it within minutes. He was the only source for that information. I wanted to visit him at his workplace one day, to see who actually took him as a model for their company. He was the main ambassador for Sara's ex-company, that I knew.

He was being a big menace to me ever since he arrived. He still ran with my book. The co-worker did not even look up at us. I tried asking for his name, but he never gave it. He was forever labelled "co-worker". It was saddening.

"You know, co-worker," I had said to him an hour after he had shown up. He did not look up at me even when I spoke to him. "A smile would be appreciated."

There had been no reaction, again. Why did I even try?

"You have been blessed with a face and the ability to make expressions. Please, use it."

Co-worker remained silent. I had given up on him, long time.

"Oliver." That was my last straw. I stared at him racing away from me for a moment. I walked over to the counter to bring the only weapon I had.

A weapon that would work really well on the boy.

Chapter 18

"Barkha."

"Oliver."

"I swear to god if you–"

"Give me my book and I won't do it. Simple."

I was amused at how Oliver had not gotten used to Dot yet. The amount of cuteness he held could make anyone fall at his small paws in obedience. If Dot wanted water, give it to him right away. If Dot said "meow", he meant it. Oliver was a lot more comfortable with Snow, Sara's cat. If his definition of comfortable still meant staying 6 feet away from it. He claimed it was because Snow was a very calm thing. Dot, a few days after I adopted him, had turned into Satan's pawn. He had a fixed battery inside him that never lost charge. He always dashed around from one place to another. The regular customers had gotten used to it. They even threatened to take him with them, for they had fallen for Dot's charms as well. Dot only ever sat still when he was asleep. He was asleep in my hands as I carried him to Oliver.

My weapon, Dot, was a serious threat to Oliver. It made him drop my book immediately, giving up. "Okay. Here. I dropped it. Take your darn book. Leave me alone."

I was satisfied with his response. It was true that he had given the book back to me, but his reaction to an asleep Dot was so funny to me that I wanted to tease him more.

With an evil smirk, I advanced to him. The more steps I took, the more he did– away from me.

"Barkha!" He groaned. "Please. I will never forgive you for this."

"Oh my god, I feel so intimidated," I said sarcastically. Had these words been said by Sara, I would have trembled.

"You do not want to know what I would do if you came even a step closer," he attempted another scare.

"Shiver me timbers."

"I'll send you back to India, I swear!" He yelped. I was already on my way back to the counter to put Dot down. I had enough satisfaction.

"Please, it took me a lot of courage to run away."

I stopped. He stopped. The co-worker stopped. The co-worker actually just stopped doing anything because there were no more customers in the mart to bill. He paid no attention or interest to what we spoke.

"Barkha…what?"

There, I had let it out. Oliver was officially the second person in town to know about my oh-so-miserable story of my journey from India to Australia. Even Mr. Co-worker did not stay to hear it, or it would make him the third person. He had scurried off to the restroom.

Since I had already told everything, I decided to tell him the real reason for me to shift there. Oliver was beyond surprised. He remained silent even after I had finished talking. I would have been, too, if I were someone else. It wasn't everyday that someone ran away from home.

"So, you see. That's how important writing is, to me," I explained, grabbing my notebook. "I'll let you read it soon enough. After my first draft." I told him the same thing I had told Sara. Ideally, I would let someone read it only after I finished it completely. The three of them, plus Liza, were exceptions.

"…Oliver?"

He stared at the floor, not saying anything to me. He looked like…he wanted to get words out, but he didn't know how to.

"You don't have to–"

"It was my father," he cut me off.

"Huh?"

"The man you saw in the shop the other day. My father. My own, biological father."

"Wait…" I took a few moments to process it. It couldn't be…

"Arch?" I asked him. He showed a startled expression, probably surprised I still remembered his name. The same mysterious man I was so curious about.

"Yes. That's my father."

Both of us needed to sit down for what he was about to say.

"My father…no, my parents always went on business trips. They loved me, don't get the wrong idea. It was work that kept them away from me. I lived with my grandparents for my entire life, with my parents visiting once every two years or so. And then…" he trailed off.

Oliver did not look me in the eye even once during the course.

"I was thirteen when they stopped visiting altogether. Either of them. I didn't know the reason then. I later found out that they had fought with each other, and stopped talking completely," he let out a gruff laugh.

"And then?"

He shrugged. "And then what, they informed my grandparents about their divorce and pshhh. Over. I continued to live with my grandparents. Both of my parents told us that they weren't ready to take me with either of them yet, that they weren't in the right mental space to do so. I completely understood them."

"This man I was so awkward with randomly showed up a month before you did, I think. In this town. He told me that my mother had remarried and had children. He was unemployed– fired from his job, even. Sam offered him a furniture shop and he took it. Sam actually helped him a lot. My father lives with us, but I barely get to see him. Because he practically just lives in the shop. So…yeah. In the end I'm still awkward with him because it's been a few months only since he came."

Co-worker walked out a second after Oliver spoke. Did he hear Oliver? No one would ever know. He had escaped the mart, mumbling something about an emergency.

I patted Oliver's shoulder. "I'm so sorry you had to go through all that. It must have been hard."

"It wasn't, to be honest. I have very loving grandparents and I'm more than happy with them. I just have to improve my relationship with my father. He's trying his best to get close to me, I can see it every time he talks to me. My mother…well, I honestly don't know. But I'm less affected by it than you think."

"If you need anything, call me," I told him.

He started to laugh. "Why, you'll be my mother? Worry about yourself first, Ms Barkha. And take that thing off the counter."

"Only if you take your nose off my business."

If I came to think of it, I knew nothing about Oliver's family before he told me. Sara's and Aaron's I had even visited, but he had never spoken about his. At least, I was glad he could trust me enough to tell me.

And out of nowhere, a hand grabbed mine and pulled me away. I could only see Oliver. He did nothing about it– he stared, that was all he did. When she let go of my hand did I realise that it was no one but the Arora daughter herself. I scrunched my eyebrows at her, she raised hers. I raised my eyebrows, and she scrunched hers. We were outside the mart before I could make sense of anything. She was out of breath. She turned around and pointed at my car, pulling on the handle even though she was aware that the car was locked.

"What?" I finally asked.

"Quick, I need to show you something. Get in."

It was not a request, it was an order.

"But– the counter is left unattended," I argued. Sara did not seem to care one bit. She was impatient and fidgety.

"Oliver is there to manage it."

I took a breath in. "I repeat, the counter is left unattended."

"Come on, Barkha. There are no customers right now. It'll be quick."

The poor Birchfield was getting abused by Sara, who continued to play with the handle.

I agreed and got in the car. Sara was about to drive.

It was the first time she sat in the car that she gave me. I remembered being so happy on the first day there. I had not only travelled miles away from home, I also bought a house at a relatively cheap price, *and* received a car as a bonus? A job, as well. I attended a party and gotten coronated by two random ladies in front of everybody. What a rollercoaster of a day, it was. All the sad emotions I had felt when I just arrived in the airport had disappeared in a flash. When I met Liza and Philip, I hated it. I had old people as neighbours and I wasn't even able to make friends. I must have been out of my mind to think that about them.

Though I was proud of myself for coming this far in life– I was enjoying my freedom and all– one thing constantly bugged me. Sara Arora. The fact that she handed me a job that easily was not surprising, since it was only a mart job. It needed no qualification whatsoever. Maybe a little English speaking skills to communicate with the customers in case they had queries. That was it. It was the fact that she handed me a car so *easily* that made me question her. Sure, I had asked for the job in the first place, so I was expected to be there. But what if I had changed my mind after she gave me the car? What if I had run away with the car? She didn't charge any money for that either. I had received it because I was an official employee. When I arrived late on my first day of work, how was I coming late the only thing that she was worried about? What if I hadn't showed up at all?

Sara shook her head, face-palming herself. "You know that I'm not that stupid. Why would I just hand over a car to you on your first day here? I didn't even know what kind of a person you were."

"That's my question exactly!"

"Barkha, I did not tell you this earlier, but every car has a tracker. Every car *owned* by my dad's employee…because they get it complementarity. We don't mean to stalk you or anything. It just shows us how far the car goes. I knew where you were on your first day of your job." It made more sense.

I did not know where she had taken me, but we had entered a five-storied building. She pressed the button for the lift and got in. I followed her.

"I wanted to show my first stitched dress to you. No, not just show it. I want you to try it on."

Chapter 19

"Why do you love me so much?"

"You're delusional, mate."

"No, why *do* you love me so much? It makes sense though. I'm naturally loveable."

"Will you ever shut up about it?"

If there was anything in life that I was proud of, it was the fact that I got both Sara and her mother to befriend me within a month of meeting them. There were perks of being friends with a rich person, and I didn't feel the least bit of shame saying it out loud. They could give out cars for free, one could get invited to their big mansion and also get a chance to look at their secret garden that no one could enter except for a few. There was also a chance they could take one to *the* event of the city near our town– also known as *the* talk of our town, that was reserved for only the special ones, and their plus ones if any. No, it wasn't a ball or prom or anything for Sara to be taking me as her plus one. If that were the case, I wouldn't let her take me either.

It was a fashion show held by one of the most famous designers in Australia. Isla Everly. Only the newborns would have not heard of the name once in their lives. At least that was what Sara told me. I, not being from Australia, was not familiar with it. On our way there, Sara kept bragging about getting invited by the designer herself to the show. I mean, who wouldn't brag.

But I also sensed a tone of sadness, or rather disappointment in her voice. Upon asking her, she told me that she had been invited because of her father's influence.

"Sure, she called me because I was a fashion designer myself. She would've invited my father otherwise, and he has no interest in fashion. The offer would ultimately have been rejected by him. If only Isla Everly recognized me as an independent designer and invited me whether or not my father was rich…" her voice lowered.

We had an extra hour and a half to pass before the show started. Sara decided to use it economically by taking me to the city's most popular tourist place.

Sara told me that she had visited the city, Radiant Ridge, many times herself, since all big events happened there. The city had a mood completely different from the town we lived in, with the bustling lives lead by people, and the rush of vehicles around us. Urban life was definitely alive-r. While Radiant Ridge resembled NYC in relation to the big buildings and constant traffic, one thing could catch the eyes of everyone all around the city. The biggest fountain in the country lay in the small city. Right at the center of it. The fountain was originally built to serve as a comfortable background sound to distract the citizens of their otherwise "monotonous" or "boring" lives in Radiant Ridge. It was made to resemble a beautiful waterfall, with stones placed in the same way. Although, I doubted anyone could even hear the water running, for the sounds of their honks were louder and much more in quantity.

The fountain lay just beside the huge hall that was to accommodate the show. The hall was huge itself, with its exteriors filled with colourful mural art depicting dancers, singers and performers.

"This hall never changed, I've been here since I was a child," Sara said as we walked up the stairs to the show.

"In two years, I imagine you up there," I whispered to Sara when Isla Everly entered the stage to welcome her guests. Everyone erupted in cheers. Sara had got the front seats on the left side of the runway. Sara told me with excitement that she wouldn't need her contact lenses either to watch, and had left it at home.

"You even had me try out your first ever dress. Who would do that?" I asked, still stuck up on the Sara loving me so much part.

Sara had designed a silk, orange-ish, skin fit dress that had me obsess over it the second I saw it. A single, big butterfly so elegantly lay beside both the arms of the dress, covering the bust. The dress was simple otherwise—it was the butterfly that caught my eyes. I continuously complimented her all the way back to the mart. We had shamelessly stopped at a restaurant to grab our afternoon teas before heading back to the mart. What could we do, we Indians had learnt that *chai* was a part of us. We couldn't miss it for the life of us. Though, I wasn't that big of a fan of the tea they sold in the town. It was rather…Australianized. There was nothing like the taste of your own country's tea. The vibe, the *feeling* I had when I drank tea in India was the reason I enjoyed drinking it. Tea in Australia didn't give me as much pleasure.

"I only wish I could design clothes as good as Isla Everly," Sara sighed. "She is the god, she's on another level."

"Hey! Don't devalue yourself. You design *amazing* dresses too," I reassured.

She laughed at me. "Are you trying to comfort me?"

"Well…" I said sheepishly.

"Isla Everly creates *haute couture* dresses," she made a frame with her fingers in exaggeration. I had no idea what that meant, but I didn't make the effort to ask. I just pretended to understand her.

"They're one of a kind, really. I truly believe Isla was gifted with the magic touch when she was born. *Every* dress she presents is a work of art. *Masterpieces.* The way she plays with patterns and shapes and *yet* perfectly matches with the modern trends is just–"

The commentator interrupted her by introducing Isla Everly's first piece. Honestly, like Sam, I did not have as much interest in fashion as Sara wanted me to. As a kid, I was always the last to know about the trends happening at the time. Whether it be the cringeworthy hair partition with the awkward side bangs, or the hairstyle with a puff. Whether it be the extremely ripped jeans or the 'pout' pose for a picture. I was disappointed when classmates made fun of me for still following 'old' trends and not getting with the new ones then, but I was actually pretty proud of myself for doing so as I sat to watch the fashion show.

Models took turns to show off Isla's 'works of art', as Sara claimed. Sara couldn't stop slapping my shoulder as she watched them come and go. While she was focused on the dresses– fangirling over each one of them– I was more focused on the models. How in the world did they maintain a poker face throughout the show? Was Mr. co-worker…a former model?!

Sara sat at the edge of her seat, mesmerized. Her mouth was open– gaping at the outfits both men and women adorned. I was drawn to the elegance each model carried with them, as if it were a piece of cake.

And then, as the show continued, a familiar figure entered from backstage. I had to squint my eyes to figure out *who* the figure was. It was a celebrity, I guessed. I turned to look at Sara in that brief second to see her squinting at the stage too– her reaction different from what she had toward other models.

"No way…" Sara whispered.

"It can't be…"

It was. The model we found so familiar was none other than our own model boy…Oliver. Unlike his usual menace of a character, he possessed a different look on his face. It was as if some spirit had gone into him for him to look so professional. The only trait that remained in him was his overflowing confidence.

But how? When? *What?* I had many questions to ask him.

"Why didn't you tell us?!" I started off. He came to us with a grin as soon as the show ended. With the way he smiled so mischievously, I realised that he knew we were coming.

Sara slapped his back hard. He showed a great reaction, immediately jolting away and holding his back in pain. "Ouch, what was that for?"

"How come you didn't tell any of us? It's not like you. You go on telling everyone even if a person complimented you."

Oliver scoffed at us. "As good friends, the ideal question should have been 'Oliver, I'm so proud of you! How did you come here'?"

When neither of us replied to that, he continued speaking.

"I will answer that first. Isla was looking for models and mind me, *one* spot was empty. Someone who had previously filled the spot had suddenly gotten into an accident– may they recover well– and she had to find one immediately. She asked around photographers for referrals, and guess who got picked, mate!" He pointed at himself repeatedly, like it wasn't obvious.

"Sam called me the other day. He got to know about me getting into *Isla Everly's* show and wanted to congratulate me, because I was going from the town, representing it in a way. He told me that he was sending his daughter and her new friend with her...so, yeah. I wanted to keep it a surprise. How was I?"

"Crikey! You absolute sly fox, which soul possessed you for you to keep a secret for so long?" Sara exclaimed, hugging him.

"Who told you I kept it a secret? Aaron knew about it. That bloke, didn't care a bit when I pitied him for not being able to come like you guys did."

It was my turn to hug him, lost as they spoke in the Aussie-est tone and accent.

"You did great up there, Oliver. I'm so proud of you," I spoke normally.

"Now, who's excited for the after-party?!" The announcer shouted, while the audience responded with cheers.

Sara had mentioned of it before, when we were in the car. Her father had appointed a driver for us, making us sit in the most luxurious car he owned. A completely black one, with windows covered with reflective film. I felt like an actual celebrity, more than Sara did. Even though I was her plus one.

I had been in her house for the whole day. The first thing I did in the morning after washing up was race to there. Well, not *actually* race. My house was pretty far to hers. Or it wasn't. I wouldn't know, the town's mentality about distances had grown on me like creepers. I refused to go anywhere without my car. Walking short distances *tired* me, in fact. It was horrible. I was slowly losing all my stamina.

She helped me pick out one of her dresses. Sara wanted to keep a good first impression with the famous designer, for me and her both. Of course she did. It was an industry she was part of, after all. With her quitting her job and starting her own brand, she was at a dangerous position. Her impression would be mistaken, people might have started to look down on her. They would blame her more than the company she quit, since they did not know her yet.

Amidst all the panic and rush Sara had, I could only think about one thing. It was completely unrelated to anything. Even Sara was taken aback by the sudden question I asked her.

"Could you maybe show me your father's car collection?"

Chapter 20

The doors opened with a loud sound, making it much more dramatic than it was. Unlike the shutter door that usually welcomed one at the entrance of a garage, Sara's had two doors as big as an elephant's body. The garage was located at the back of the house, completely covered from the front by the humongous house itself. It was only two feet or so shorter than the actual house, and just as wide. But only those who got to visit it knew how far the single garage extended.

The view was extraordinary. A mall's parking lot would have had lesser cars than Sam Arora. It was amusing. Not only was the garage spacious, it also contained hundreds of cars within it. I did not expect to see the number of cars, even if I was prepared for it mentally. And when I said *hundreds* of cars, I meant it. All kinds of cars existed– from the ones that prevailed before Birchfield to the newest ones.

"The old ones aren't available for selling," Sara explained to me, running her hand through a *Checker*. Though it was old, it had no rust or dust on it whatsoever. Sam must really love his cars to be able to maintain it so properly. I heard from his daughter that he didn't allow any of the maids of the house in the garage either, in fear of his cars getting stolen.

"How did you give me an old model, then?"

"Employees only. It might sound rude but dad doesn't give it for free just like that, he'll claim it back when or if they get fired or end up quitting. Then, you can purchase a car of a newer brand."

It was all too exciting for me. Aaron was right, Sam Arora was an incredible man. And his actual job was nowhere related to cars. He simply happened to have great interest in cars.

"Then why does he sell the cars at cheap rates?"

Sara laughed sheepishly. "Because the people that buy it for cheaper rates promise to stay within the town. Ultimately, the cars still belong to my dad. It's more like they rent the cars, until they move out, if they do. If they don't…well, they get cars too, and my father gets money too. It's a win-win situation."

"And what if they want the car even after they move out? Can they pay more to get it?"

"I mean, if the car is something that dad doesn't *need* in his inventory. Each car is important to him. I wouldn't know, it hasn't happened before."

Given the population of the town to be easily more than a thousand– with almost every house owning a car from Sam Arora's collection– how many would he actually be owning?

"Barkha. Barkha. Barkha. Barkha."

"You'll be fine! Calm down," I told a nervous Sara. She fidgeted with her dress.

"I don't want to miss this opportunity. But I don't feel like talking."

The DJ during the after-party was bomb, he played all kinds of music. I need not mention how good the food was. *Everything* was served. Literally. I was so surprised to see a stall that sold *pani puri* too. I made a decision to live there forever.

"Make it spicier, sir, what is this? It's so sweet," I grumbled, ignoring Sara's constant whining.

"Sara, trust me. She's right there. If you don't go, I will."

She denied immediately. "No. I'll go." She headed off to the famous designer, who was already engaged in a conversation. Isla noticed her presence and excused herself from her current conversation, to pay attention to what Sara had to say.

"This is the spiciest I can go, ma'am," the man at the counter told me, handing a puri to me.

It was spicy for sure, but not the type of spicy a regular pani puri should be. No, it tasted like an extremely spicy chili powder instead. So much for wondering why the insides of the puri had suddenly changed its colour to red.

"What did you put in?!" I intended for it to be a rhetorical question.

"You said you wanted your pani puri spicy," he argued, snatching the bowl from me in annoyance. "You don't have to eat it anymore, ma'am."

"Learn how to pronounce 'pani puri' properly first, Gora—"

"Okay, I'll take her with me…" Oliver appeared out of nowhere. It was the first time I saw him at the party that night. As soon as the three of us had entered the room, he disappeared in the pool of other models, who were supposedly his friends.

'Do you think Sara's doing okay?" He asked me. I scrunched my eyebrows at him.

"Why wouldn't she be okay?"

He made me turn my head to a direction to face Sara and Isla. Her body posture had completely changed. She slouched down, clearly attempting to hide her face. Isla had taken off the smile from her face and replaced it with a mixture of anger and confusion. She turned around, kept her nose in the air and walked away.

Oliver and I ran to Sara's side.

"Hey, what happened?" I patted her back as Oliver searched to see where Isla had gone.

"My boss. He got to know I was coming here. Apparently, he's close friends with the entire industry. That man called Isla up and spread misinformation about me. Can you believe that he told her that I was disobedient, and when he tried to teach me how things were done, I got angry and quit the company? How cruel can a person be!" She wasn't crying, but I knew she wanted to. I could tell by the shaky breath she took in.

"I tried to explain to her that it wasn't true and that he was lying. Did she care to listen to me? Not one bit. Why is life so unfair…"

The first thing I did then was pull Sara into a hug. Oliver joined in.

"I am so sorry, Sara," I muttered.

She smiled. "If you were the one who created the problem for me, I wouldn't even be speaking to you now. You have nothing to be sorry about. Now, I just found the motivation to work on my shop. I'll prove to them that I'm innocent. I'll get famous not because I'm Sam Arora's daughter, but as a designer. I'll become famous worldwide. More than Isla Everly. My brand will be called 'Sara Arora' and *every* elite person will have at least one design of mine in their houses. I promise this."

Oliver shouted a cheer, not caring about people's eyes on him as he did. "And I will no longer be just a replacement. I'll be called to shows in a flash. I'll become the ambassador for the biggest companies. The designer brands will invite *me* to all their shows. I promise this!"

I was energized. If the two of them harboured big ambitions, why couldn't I? My parents always told me to aim high, to dream big. Even though their idea of my big dream was completely different, I still made use of their advice then.

"And I!" I began, my voice not louder than the music being played. "I will have completed my novel by the end of this year and published it. I will become a best-selling author. Everybody will love my book. I promise this."

The three of us escape a good party to go back to the grand fountain. The Sara an hour before we came out of the party would be so mad, but the new Sara did not care.

"If you chuck a coin into this, your wish comes true. At least that's what I have heard," she said to us. Usually, these superstitions and beliefs didn't get into my head. My mother was queen bee when it came to superstitions. I don't know where she heard what, but when it came to whatever I did, she found a wrong in it– scolding me for not following her beliefs.

She used to make me stand under a shelter filled with crows. Drag me early in the morning. While I used to cry about the fear of a bird pooping on me, that was exactly what my mother wanted. "It should poop on you, it brings good luck to you," she told me. She wouldn't leave me until it actually happened.

She used to throw a black cloth on the mirror in the bathroom every morning. The cloth was gone after every member of our small family took bath. Then the next morning, it appeared again. I made a mistake of asking her why she did so, because I received a ridiculous answer. "You should not see your face in the morning. Your day will be bad." She knew I wouldn't listen to her if she told me to not look without the cloth being there. That was why she put one.

Another time, I had made myself Maggi. *Maggi* was an emotion as a child, I missed it so much. God knows if it was available in the town. Since I was alone in the house, I did not want to wash another utensil. I ate in the vessel I cooked the noodles in. When my mother got back, she beat my back. "Who told you to eat in that? It will rain at your wedding!" I was fourteen then, so far from getting married. Little did they know I would escape from marriage altogether. My mother must have been blaming all the bad things I did as a child, as I threw a coin into the fountain. A dollar was wasted, but it did not affect me. I was too high on motivation. We all were. We left the city right then to get back into the town.

Aaron was flabbergasted the next day, when he heard that all of us left the party to work. Oliver watched videos to better his poses, and did his skincare. Sara started to sketch endlessly until she found a design that satisfied her. I wrote 1500 words without a break, which was my biggest accomplishment ever.

Chapter 21

"Why not!"

"Sara, I'm not interested."

"But that's the whole experience–"

"Well, then I do not want to have the experience, leave me alone."

A month later, Sara had already submitted twenty of her designs to the tailor company. She would open the shop after every dress was stitched, in another month. She was the most excited about it. The previous month, she had gone very hard on herself. Something in her had changed after the fountain incident. It got me wondering if the belief that our wishes would come true was actually true. But it couldn't be. I was still stuck on one sentence. It had been three days already, and I had made no progress. The only way I could finish it in the year (which was nine months to go) was if I sat for two months straight to complete it, without going to the mart once or getting even a little distracted. I knew myself– I would relax for seven months, without completing much. Then I would start to get stressed and force myself to write, even if the quality of the book was trash. It had happened to me before, back in India. Though I had no pressure of publishing it then.

To save me the stress of later, I decided to take the stress right then. *Amazing plan, Barkha.* The fact that Sara was pestering me in the mart did not help me.

The mart had become our house. Over the course of one month, Aaron had felt left out since he had no other hobby but to cook. He needed to continue cooking, but he couldn't because of his mart job. Sara had an idea for that as well.

"How about…you open a stall outside the mart? You could sell *anything*. From Dampers to actual meals. It's a new section of the mart– think of it that way. You would earn more money as well."

"And what, would the mart be left vacant? Barkha alone would not be able to handle the customers," Aaron argued, though the idea of having his own stall excited him. We could all see it in his eyes.

"I'll just call David again. He was asking for a job availability anyway," she said nonchalantly.

"Who's David?" I asked. It was a name I had not heard before.

Sara gasped. "You worked with him! You didn't have the decency of asking him for his name?"

I had worked with someone? There was no one I had worked with apart from Aaron and…

No way…

I burst out laughing. "Mr. Co-worker?"

The rest of them were confused, especially because Oliver wasn't there to laugh with me.

"I just…didn't ask him," I giggled, letting my encounter with co-worker remain a mystery. To be honest, I did not want him to have a name. I would continue to call him by the endearing title I had given to him.

"Anyway, Aaron, what do you say?"

A month later, there he stood– selling meat pies that he prepared on the spot for his customers. The business was booming already. I was just upset that I couldn't eat the pie– I was a vegetarian. Aaron also sold brownies in the same stall. I had sworn I hadn't tasted better brownies in my life– excluding Liza's. Hers was a different story in itself.

Damper man, upset about another man selling bigger than him, moved away. I kind of missed him and the constant rushes to the mart everyday to avoid buying the breads. Okay, I wasn't that cruel– I even *bought* his bread once. He was overjoyed. But I did not enjoy it as much as I had enjoyed Aaron's.

Sara wanted to build a comfortable space for me to write as well. She was to give the empty room connecting to her garden to me, to use as my own writing corner. While I appreciated her love for me, I found it ridiculous.

"Sara, I'm here to do my job as a mart employee. Why would I do anything else but bill customers during my work? This mart is always full, now that there's a stall too. Let me do my work peacefully. I have all the time to write as soon as I'm off work."

She scoffed. "This is the first time I've seen someone so willing to work at a mart."

I wasn't willing to work there. I just didn't want to disrespect her and the Arora house. If I was doing something, I had to do it with full dedication. What was the point of coming to work if all I did was write, and unwillingly bill the groceries bought by the customers? The job could go to another person instead, and I could sit and home and write how much ever I wanted to. I liked the sound of the idea, but at the same time, I needed money.

I explained it to Sara.

"Why do you carry that handbook with you here, then? To write!" She was angry at me because I was working at a mart her family owned?

"Sara, it's been so long since I've even written in this. The mart is so busy. Now, go away unless you want to buy something from here. Have you checked out the new range of toothpastes, ma'am? It has cars on them! I think it would suit you."

She tsked and walked out of the door after looking at me one last time. "I'm off to design. Enjoy your mart work."

Autumn had tip-toed its way to the town. I was spelled by the beauty of it. The trees were coloured emerald, golden and orange at the same time. The humid weather had finally come to an end, replaced quickly by cool breeze, brushing through everyone so delicately. I simply loved the weather.

Mahen hated the weather. He hated stepping outside of his house. It didn't make much of a difference if he did too, for his house was just as cold as the weather outside. One like him should have been extremely happy and fortunate, but Mahen felt neither of those emotions…for quite a long time. He still had to buy milk for himself. Mahen made his way outside– not bothering to slip a sweater on him. The street was completely deserted. His empty, lonely, dying heart felt a pang in it, crumbling for the umpteenth time as his eyes roamed around the abandoned shops. He let it crumble. He let it crumble with the dry leaves under his feet.

He couldn't complain. He wanted to tear apart the throat of the person that left him in this state– body the width of paper, from not eating as much. Cheeks fully sucked in. His skeletal structure prominently seen popping out.

He wanted to tear apart his own throat, for it was he himself who had turned him into a skeleton. The dry leaves flew up in the air, afraid of being crushed by Mahen's feet. With the leaves flew his will to survive.

What had he done? What had Mahen become? Where was the coward in him, that could have stopped all of his doings within a second? What had gotten into him, for him to have quite literally end the lives of every factory worker?

He was not that cruel. It wasn't him that did it. It couldn't be. Mahen was a nice boy. He was obedient and foolish. His brain was empty. He was a jolly man. Everybody loved Mahen.

Everybody loved him.

Everybody.

Where was everybody? Where had they disappeared? If they loved him so much, why did they not help him?

Didn't loving people usually help out, when one was in a troubled state?

Did they not help one out, afraid of what would happen to them?

Did...no one even care about Mahen anymore? No one at all?

No, people cared about him. They resided in big houses. They had moustaches half the size of their heads. They sat in a building full of terrifying rooms. Terrifying rooms full of maniacs like Mahen. They had illegally colonized Mahen's entire country.

They cared enough about him to be looking for him. Out in the hunt of the responsible person. To punish him to death.

But, at least they were looking for him. Did everybody else do that?

Mahen felt shivers in his body. Not because of the cold weather, but because of the emptiness of his heart. Because of the lingering cool air after the fire in his heart was extinguished. The warmth he enjoyed not too long ago had disappeared. The candle that the fire was lit on was taken away. The table that held the candle was collecting dust, as if that was what it was meant to be doing. Mahen felt another pang in his heart— like it was squeezing itself for any trace of warmth. His heart was empty, so Mahen fell to the ground.

I rose from the ground, cursing Louis with my face. He responded with laughter.

"What kind of a kid are you, not giving your elders any respect?"

He mumbled my words again, mimicking me. He received a slap on the neck for that.

"Sorry, sorry. My leg just happened to be in your way. You just happened to trip on it."

I brushed the grass off my jeans. "You're lucky the ground was soft," I rolled my eyes at him.

"Now come on, we're getting late! I told you to come with me. You didn't listen, and now we're late," he complained.

"Forgive me for working to live. And we aren't late, we have 30 minutes left with us. I could go back home and come here and we would still be early."

We were in the town's most famous college. If the hall next to the grand fountain was that city's main house of formal events, the Magnolia Academy was the town's.

I was as excited as Gertrude was about the event, because it concerned both of us, and none of my other friends.

The VerseGala was a literary-theatre-film fest. It included everything, from the screening of short films, to authors showing up for seminars, to various performances of drama or theatre. To Louis and me, it was heaven. He told me about it one day before Liza did.

"Barkha, open up!" He had knocked on my door at 12 in the night like some creep. Fortunately for him, I was very much awake and breaking my head to continue writing the book. Though, he wasn't lucky enough to escape Philip.

If Sam Arora was the head of the town, Philip was his father. Not literally, of course.

"Who is that creating ruckus at this time? Oliver!"

Poor Oliver was always going to get blamed.

After telling me of the fest, he ran away to his own house. His mother must be too relaxed and trust her son so much to be able to send him out so freely. I did not wish that I roamed at night as a child, but freedom sounded good.

Liza informed me the next day— she said that Jimmy Brown was going to be there, and I couldn't miss it for the life of me. Not like I was planning to.

At 12 a.m. after Louis had told me, I messaged Sara about not being available on that afternoon at the mart.

"I must act as your guardian. You will not go anywhere without telling me first. Now, come to Jimmy Brown's talk with me. You can split later on."

I was not planning to take any risk. The event was huge, and Louis could get lost anywhere. He told me that he was going to meet his friends later and even gave their numbers to me, but if I couldn't trust him, how could I trust his friends?

His mother had come to me before I had left for work that morning, as though I had manifested her by thinking about her. It was the first time I ever spoke to her, or even just greeted her. I couldn't recognize her for a while.

"Take care of my son, please. I know he's grown enough to roam freely without getting lost, but he is still a child. My son speaks highly of you, so I am putting my full trust in you. You can let him go around to different events, but check up on him every once in a while. Thank you," she had grasped my hands and pulled out a box of chocolates. She smiled at me, her face shining as bright as the Sun. It made me smile back instantly.

"My husband got this from the US. Please have it. It's the least I can do for you, in return of you feeding Louis the other day and for today."

I walked with Louis in the college with a hand wrapped around his shoulder.

Chapter 22

"Australia is having a great weather today, no?" The voice in the radio said.

It wasn't just the weather that was great. Everything about that day was. From waking up early in the morning to go for a jog, to being motivated to write 2000 words already. I was so happy, I decided to *cook*.

Cooking was something I had no expertise in…at all. I had never learnt it as a child. I went to school, came back, slept, studied, wrote if I could, ate and slept again. Those were pretty much the only things I did.

To impress our parents, Avi and enrolled ourselves in a cooking competition at school. Our previously boring school, suddenly wanted to update in our last year there. It was like they hated our batch, or something. Art, cooking, dance and singing were suddenly added in our annual day celebration, making every student look forward to the day more. The school was evil. Right after the annual day, they would announce the dates for our final exams. That year, we were to sit for boards.

"Let's do something different," Avi snickered.

"I am not going to cook, Avi. You want me to burn the school down, or what?"

"It's happening outside, idiot. And you know how to make Maggi. I've already given your name to ma'am," he ran.

"Avyukt, I swear to god."

A good school that had responsibility of their students would have kept it a 'cooking without fire' competition. Ours had no shame, I thought.

I ran home to my mother. She was impressed, much to my surprise. The woman who despised if I woke up late, if I slept early and if I pretty much did anything but study, was happy that I got into a cooking competition.

"I will teach you how to make *Vada Pav*. You will break the stage with this. The judges will love you. If they do, then the teachers will come to love you too. You will get better marks! You will become the MVP!"

How was one to learn a dish in less than a day, especially an inexperienced one? My mother taught me to make it all night. I perfected it…only after twenty tries…and only to forget it the next day.

Luckily, I had got a packet of instant noodles with me. Just in case. In mere pressure, that was exactly what I ended up cooking. The look on my mother's face when she found out was unmatchable. I kind of felt bad for her, for she spent so much of her time on me, and it all went to waste.

Avi laughed at me the whole journey home. "Shut up," I kicked the back of his knees, making him bend awkwardly.

"You could have at least *attempted* to make the Vada Pav. Making Maggi is ridiculous," he exclaimed.

"Hey, it was your idea," I laughed with him. Looking back at it, it was *actually* ridiculous. Though the judges' reaction when they saw my dish made it all worth it.

The two of us made our way to our favourite spot— the lakeside. It had the best of my memories. I showed Avyukt my first manuscript there, and he had complimented me endlessly— threatening me that he would publish it if I didn't. In the end, I did not publish it. My parents were against it, they said to focus on my studies instead. Like a good child, I obeyed them.

I was then snapped out of my thoughts by a splash of water. I turned to look at an evil boy with an evil grin. Avi tried to escape, but I caught up with him and got my revenge. Revenge was always sweet.

"Sorry, sorry," he chuckled.

"But I don't understand," I said to him then, dusting the sand off my slippers. "You haven't even stepped into the kitchen, how did you manage to win the competition?"

He showed me a smirk. "You know, sometimes, it's better if you take the easy way…"

I tilted my head in confusion. "What…" I trailed off when I saw his fingers, mimicking the counting of money. "No, you didn't!" I gasped.

"No, I didn't," he replied casually. "I realised I'm just good at cooking naturally, I can't help it. At this rate, I'd become a chef in the future."

"What do you really want to become?" I asked in a serious tone.

"A pilot. I feel like I suit the job the best." His smile faded from my vision, replaced quickly by a concerned passerby.

"Mate, be careful there. You don't want to kill someone with your car, do ya? It looks expensive too," he tutted at me and walked away.

AV's voice continued to play on the radio. I realised I had not been listening to it for a single second. "…he said that, and I thought about it. If he were the established cook in our dorm, why could he not continue being one, right? I always do the laundry. It's unfair on me to be cooking, too. Please, listeners, find us a way to get rid of this childish banter. With that note, listen to our song 'Chatter' now, before we end the radio for the day. Thank you..." his voice trailed off and hype song started to play. Cooking. What a coincidence...

I had to travel far to grab Indian ingredients, since it wasn't in our mart. And by far, I mean to Sara's house. It's the nearest supermarket after ours, with Poonam Aunty as the shopkeeper.

"Thank you so much!" I told her when she handed me the ingredients that she had already placed in a cloth bag.

She didn't smile from her eyes. "Are you sure you'll be fine alone? You're saying it's your first time trying a dish like this... And you're inviting my daughter. Do I have the assurance that she won't be poisoned?"

I clutched my chest with a gasp. "Aunty, is this what you think of me?"

"Go, go. Enjoy," she smiled.

Although a joke, I rethought about what aunty said. I had the ability to poison them.

If there were several reasons to run away from home, food was *not* one to be included. I absolutely scarfed down all the food my mother used to cook for us. I only wished I had the gene passed down from my mother.

I was beginning to regret everything, but I certainly could not cancel it. I had done everything– made a big deal out of it, bragged about my cooking skills to Louis *only* in defense to him mocking me, invited everyone I was close with, told Poonam Aunty that she was going to miss my cooking big time *and* even named the little get-together: Barkha Welcoming Party.

I knew, I knew. I knew that the whole town had already crowned me and applauded me for the only reason being I was a new addition to the town– which meant another person paying tax 6 months after staying there, and another earning person in town.

But…I felt like *I* never once thanked them enough for welcoming me so grandly– and making conversations with me so freely, every single one of them. I half expected most of them to have a typical stereotype towards Indians. I didn't know if it was because Sara had Indian roots, but they treated me like one of their own, from the start. Whether it be the urbane Philip or the crude young boy Louis. That, or I just wanted people around me since I was feeling quite lonely the past few days.

No one could blame me for feeling so; Sara rarely made visits to the mart anymore because she was so caught up with her designing. Oliver visited even lesser– he had joined a modelling course one town away. Aaron was quite literally outside the mart all the time, but that drifted us apart. I missed the laughs we shared occassionally, while billing the customers. They sometimes thought that we needed a mental asylum. Liza was busy with everything and anything that was happening in town. And by anything, I *meant* anything– an unknown person leaving her baby in Liza's care or Liza offering to help at cafes, though she was not a regular worker. She could– I was not exaggerating– do *anything* and the town would not say a word against it. In fact, even Philip had a soft spot towards her, he looked at her like a daughter.

"Need help?"

"Maybe just a little," I told Sara with a grunt. In front of me, I had four cookbooks given by her mother, and in my hand a phone with a million open tabs on Google. All containing recipes. That day, I was determined enough to feed all of them a full meal. Starters, main course, desserts– everything. Although I depended on Liza for the dessert and Aaron for the starter.

Roti, Egg Curry, Dal Makhani. Paneer Tikka for starters and *Ras Malai* for dessert. What more would one need in life?

Dal Makhani was the only thing I was good at making, and made all by myself. Sara's knowledge in the kitchen helped in making the rotis as round as they could be.

"It was you who threw a ball into my window last year, was it not?" Philip grumpily asked Louis, pushing the younger's forehead away with his pointer finger. He covered in fear and shook his head vigorously.

"Not me, not me."

"Barkha…I think you might have found yourself a new thing you're good at. This is *amazing*!" I didn't know then if Oliver was sugarcoating it, neither did I pay it any attention. The people that lived in India and ate that on a monthly basis would have had different opinions on my cooking, but I did not care. I had received a compliment, and that too in something I was the least confident about. I was not planning to create a hobby of this even after the compliments.

"Thank you, so much. I am truly honoured to be called by you, dearest one," Philip clapped his hands together. "Although the heat is killing me."

I had made the poor decision of hosting my fellow townmates on my terrace, with a portable stove and oven I had asked Oliver to borrow from his father.

"You fool, I asked you to bring your father along with you. Did you even tell him? How would it make me as a character if I didn't invite the main contributor to this afternoon?" I had scolded him at my front door step when he arrived to my house.

"I asked him," Oliver had shrugged. "He is not really big on coming to events like these. He is a big introvert, so…" he winced at me. "Though he promised to treat you back for it one day, and officially meet all my friends *as* my friends, not as his boss' daughter. Well, Sam is not technically his *boss*, but I didn't know how else to phrase it–"

"You talk too much," I cut him off. "Tell your father that he owes me nothing at all, but I would love to meet him 'as my friend's father', not as a furniture seller."

Oliver had gotten pretty close to his father over the month. It was heartwarming to see. He would speak about him whenever we met. While he usually ranted about the things his dad did in the mornings they saw each other, he would end it with a smile.

I hated Sara's confidence. She growled at everybody like a lion when she was confident. I was pretty confident in my game– even used to brag about it to Avi and my family as a child– until I met the mastermind. Sara.

It was like she despised me, or something, with the way her red, evil eyes shone at me. "Pick four cards up. Right now."

I turned to Liza for help. I rested my head naturally on her shoulder and pointed at Sara. "Liza, look at her. Tell her to play fairly."

Sara threw her hands in the air in disbelief. "What about this wasn't fair?"

"I don't want to sit next to you," I concluded. My seating was wrong after all. If I hadn't been sitting next to Sara, I would have had the least number of cards.

"Go easy on her, Shay. She's not as good at it as you are," Liza laughed. A smile lingered on Sara's lips at the nickname.

"Yes, exactly– wait, what?"

Good thing Louis had to run for his theatre practice. I would *not* want to watch myself lose to a child. My ego was bigger than that.

Chapter 23

"Thank you for cooking for us. I loved it. I hadn't had Indian food in so long," Liza said to me.

We were the only ones left, cleaning everything up properly. Sara told me to take rest and not come to the supermarket after lunch break, but I denied.

With the number of rest days my manager allowed me to take, at that rate I would be considered unemployed. Sara rolled her eyes at me when I said that to her. "It isn't like you aren't doing anything sitting at home. You're writing. Soon, when your book gets published, I expect you to take us everywhere." Said the girl with the most money.

"By now, you should've opened a restaurant with your amazing cooking," Liza laughed.

"I think one of us needs a restaurant more than the other."

Liza smiled warmly, but I couldn't sense the authenticity in it. Her eyes held deeper meanings that I could not decipher. "Barkha…" she started. I felt an uneasiness in my stomach for no reason. "I know you convinced Sara to open her own shop and all, and I am very proud of both of you for it. But don't try to bring the mindset into me as well. I know you've tried to, multiple times. I am old. I have enough money. Every day for me is a new one. I am always doing something or the other to entertain myself and I'm perfectly fine not doing anything as well."

I knew she didn't mean to, but her tone hit me like a dagger.

"I–I'm sorry, I didn't mean to–"

"I know you want the best for everybody. That's my favourite trait of yours. You are just like my son," she patted my back, sitting down on a chair and tapping on the one next to her. I listened to her. I felt like I knew her as a child. The level of comfort and happiness she provided me with was immense, like she was a witch who cast a spell on me.

I turned to look at her. "You have…a son? Why have you never told me that?"

In fact, I had no clue Liza was even married. Why had I never met her son?

Liza fiddled with the sleeveless kurta she wore. Wearing it and eating Indian food made her look like a complete Indian Aunty. I always loved the women who looked like her– not conservative, open, comfortable dresses and overall an amazing personality.

That was how my aunt was.

"That's what I wanted to talk about actually, with you…" Liza mumbled under her breath, almost undecipherable.

"What?" I asked calmly. The quick beating of my heart pretty much gave away that I was the opposite of calm them. Though I had heard nothing of what Liza was about to say to me, it scared me.

"My son…" she trailed off, clearing her throat. I wrapped my hand around her shoulder instinctively.

"You can take your time," I comforted her.

She gave me a smile one more time before shaking her head. "I don't have to. It's a happy thing, but it's also… Okay, I'll just say it. I rarely went to visit my son, right? He lives in Sydney. How would I get the money and time to go there?" Her face softened as she stared into nothing with a stupid smile on her face. I loved it when she could comfortably tell me about her life. It made me feel very…daughterly.

"I'll start from first, because I never have once spoken about my family to you. I think you deserve to know. You shared yours to me, trusting me completely."

She was right. I did tell Liza about my parents, much more in detail than I had to anyone in that town. She embraced me like a mother and I smiled into her arms. Running away from home was not something I cried about anymore, and it made me happy knowing that. I definitely wasn't very proud of myself for running either.

"I was married away at a quite young age. 24, to be exact. Your age. But I was happy with my husband, we lived happily for many years. A perfectly healthy son was born to us, by God's grace. I was truly blessed. Then, my son grew up and went away from home to study. My husband…well, his own heart betrayed him. I could do nothing about it. I was so hopeless, so stupid to not take him to a hospital immediately. I sat next to him and cried, for hours. My son came not long after and scolded me, shouted at me. I understood that I could have saved his life…had I taken him to the hospital. I wanted to—"

She let out a breath, and I followed her. I hadn't noticed I was holding my breath too. She was not on the verge of crying, but obviously, she didn't look happy either.

"It's okay, Barkha. It's been years since the incident. Time truly heals us, you know. Try trusting the importance of it."

"Liza…"

"I wanted to tell you that…my son called me the other day. Last month. He now has a wife and a beautiful baby together. He told me that they recently shifted to a new house— big enough to fit about five people. My son asked me to move in with him, now that he earned plenty of money *and* a promotion. I'm so incredibly proud of my boy."

In that brief moment of happiness, I hadn't realised what she really meant to say.

"Barkha, I'll be moving from here. Next week. Forever, I think. Leaving our beloved home. Finding a new one and building great memories just like I did here. It was only fair to inform you about it way before I left."

I did not know how to feel about the piece of information. Liza was someone I could always run to. In the past few months since I arrived, she took care of me the most. She was someone I could trust with my whole heart, without a doubt. The fact that I was going to lose my technical support system was…

"I know, I feel sad, too. Way more than you do. My memories of this place, the people I met. *You*. Barkha, you are the most extraordinary person I have ever met. So introverted, yet so extroverted. So moody, yet so happy. So dedicated to your job and to what you really love to do as well. So brave to run away. So ambitious—"

"Stop, already. Do you want me to cry now?" I asked her, wiping the side of my eye with a short laugh. How was it possible to get so attached to someone that quickly?

Come to think of it, I had loved her from day one. From the time we spent in the car, laughing about the residents of the town. From the time she almost broke my door to wake me up for the party. I had come a long way. We both had.

"You've decorated your house pretty well, ey?" Liza nudged me.

I didn't understand why she was trying to change the topic.

"Next week, you said? Who all know about it?"

She sighed. "Just a few of my friends. Sara and Sam, since I returned the car back to them. No one else. They'll all get to know the day before I leave, anyway."

"Why do you say so?" I asked her, genuinely curious.

She smiled sheepishly, scratching the back of her neck. "You know Sam. You know how he makes a big deal out of anything and everything… God, this is embarrassing to say out loud. They are hosting a farewell party for me."

I chuckled amidst the tense environment. "Are you that important to the town, Liza Jones?"

She joked along with me, shrugging nonchalantly before putting her nose in the air. "The effect of living long enough in this town. Everybody just comes to love me naturally, you know? I even get people I met just a few months ago *crying* for my departure."

I looked at the ground awkwardly.

"You leave all the sappy stuff aside. Today is *your* day. 'Barkha welcoming day'. Let's celebrate you. Come on, are you up for a movie marathon? I baked cookies just for you! I didn't bring it here because I didn't want those troublesome kids to steal it from you. It's *just* for you.

Chapter 24

From the way the center of the town was decorated, one would think we were welcoming a VIP. The strings they usually hung at carnivals with the triangular hangings attached to it, was hung all around town. They were right when they said the town was extreme when it came to celebrations. Anything and everything called for a party. Not like I was complaining. I agreed, the occasion we currently celebrated called for a *celebration*. Though 'celebration' was not the right word there. Liza was leaving. We commemorated her 30 years of living in the town. The main character never stopped talking to people, walking around the whole town and stopping wherever she found life. Trees included– she always stood next to one and caressed its leaves, as though she had planted and grown it herself. Maybe she actually had. If she had, I wouldn't be surprised. She was just that kind of a person.

"How much do you bet everyone's going to make a scene later today?" Sara whispered next to me. "There's going to be tears flying out of their eyes for this, I'm telling you."

"Oi, have a tender heart. Liza is…she's…" Oliver's face contorted, him almost on the verge of crying.

"Oh, don't start with it. You look terrible," Sara folded her arms and moved away from him.

Liza walked on the small stage-like platform, the mic screeching as she reached for it. It caught everybody's attention. They let out wails, cries, shouts of displeasure as they watched her. Liza was treated like a complete celebrity.

She laughed, in contrast to her teary eyes. "Shut up already, I'm not *dying*."

What shocked me was that three seats away from me, next to Sara, sat her father– wiping his eyes with a handkerchief.

"I'd like to thank each one of you for being a part of my life. With a light heart, I entered this town with my husband. I will leave the town with the same heart. And I will step into a new one, and have a very different life from this one. But that's okay, it's all part of life anyway. I don't regret anything. I certainly do not regret meeting any of you. Whether it's the babies I watched grow up," she smiled at my friends, "or the people *I* grew up with. Or even the people I met recently. But again, while I'm sad about leaving, I am looking forward to it too. What new things are awaiting me? Anyway…that's all I have to say. I'm so happy today."

Liza's departure hit me like a truck. She was just someone I knew, I wanted to tell myself. People came and went, right? I shouldn't have been so stuck on the fact that she left.

Her house looked the same from the outside, with the purple flowers and the creepers, even a month after she left. The house stood deserted, withering in silence. Not a single person came to inquire about buying the house.

I stared at the abandoned house with a million questions flooding my mind. Who owned the house I lived in, before I moved in? Did they leave with feelings similar to that of Liza's? Did the townspeople send them off in the same way? Did their departure still trouble every person in town? Did they leave the same impact on Liza as she did on me? The mysteries would forever be left unsolved. It itched my brain.

The town had a distinct difference to the gully I grew up in. Individuals in the town had clearly a warm heart, a welcoming characteristic and a good personality overall. Did they imprint it on everybody when they first arrived to the town? Was it carried by genes? The number of genuine people in my gully was less. They were rather overpowered by the number of people that judged every one of us.

While no stranger cared for one's birth or death back there, someone that had the courtesy to find out the name of a resident of the town was shaken by their death, or rejoiced the birth of their child.

I found out not a week after Liza left that they had a whole record book of the people of the town. Each time a new resident joined, another page would be added to it. I was so surprised that I had to go check it out at the public library.

The doors of the library rung in joy when I entered. Like the bells, the librarian held a warm smile on her face as soon as she saw me. "Hi, Barkha."

I had never once gone to the library, neither had I seen the woman around. How did she know my name?

"What..." I wondered out loud. Her big blue eyes widened, covering quarter of her face.

"Don't worry, I'm not your stalker!" She blurted out, when I had not even accused her of being one. "I– I mean to say. Obviously stalker wasn't the first thing that popped in my mind!"

The way she was panicking, it made me panic with her. "What," I repeated, more anxious than before.

"No, I know every resident. The record book is basically my Bible, it's so interesting as well. It's amazing how much information you'll find about yourself. They're all put by Philip and his friends. Sam, too," she explained once she had calmed down.

"So…you found me in it?"

She nodded firmly.

"Not much would be there about me, no? I just recently joined the town."

"Four months isn't very recent. Also, how did you manage to befriend Sara? Do you know…never mind," she stopped herself from speaking. Why would someone start to say something and then end it with a 'never mind'? It got on my nerves.

"Please, tell me, miss," I practically begged.

"Well, if you're one of Sara's close friends… you're considered cool, to us teenagers. Oliver, Aaron, Sara and you are basically the ideal friend group of the town– the ones we look up to the most among the people of your age here."

Only after she said that did I realise that she looked *way* younger than me.

"Oh my god," I breathed. Did people really look up to us? It was only because we were Sara's friends, of course. Yet the fact made me so jumpy.

"It's like you guys are the Power Rangers, or something. Or better, a music group that we all are fond of. I know it's a bit mindless of me to say it in front of you, but Aaron is my favourite," she admired out loud.

I was taken aback fully, and maybe she sensed it, because she stopped rambling immediately. She showed her teeth while she smiled, embarrassed. I stood in the same spot– gaping at her.

"You can…go check the books out, if that's what you came for. I mean, obviously you did. This is a library, after all. My name is Flora, by the way. Not like you asked. I should stop. You should continue."

Flora was sixteen, she told me upon further inquiry. She worked as a librarian as a side hustle, to help and earn for her family. "I switch with another woman during daytime. I take the night duty. This insomnia really helps me be awake for customers." She could've worked at a cafe instead, like most people around her age did. But her passion for reading made her a librarian. To be honest, when I was much younger than her, it was my dream job, too. Imagine– you just sit at one place filled with books *and* get to read whenever you wanted?

"I wanted to read the record book you were talking about," I said to Flora.

Her smile got bigger. She ran inside what I hoped would be a storeroom and not a secret garden. Flora walked out with a book, thicker than I expected it to be. A beautiful purple cover adorned the book, its pages perfectly bound together by book hoops.

"How long have they had this?" I asked.

"Oh, 40 years. Ever since they came into the town, started to inhabit it. Thankfully, the town has only less than a 1000 people now. They would not even have thought of making a book if there were more from the start."

I ran my hands through the cover of the book slowly. "What if they aren't able to add any more pages to this book in the future?"

'They would make a part two of it. Now that they started it, they wouldn't abandon it." Of course, what a stupid question.

The book was maintained so neatly, even after 40 years. There was not a speck of dust on it. Flora probably took utmost care of it. It was the only source of the town's history, at the end of the day.

On the first page of the book was a mid-aged man– smiling in the black and white picture of his like he had just won a lottery. The name under the picture read...

"Philip?" I laughed. I couldn't believe my eyes. Was it really the old man I knew? Come to think about it, he had mentioned that he was a handsome young man once upon a time. I refused to believe him, but I did not dare to say it in front of him. "I'm sure you did," I had squeaked. I never in my life would have thought he was actually right.

Philip, for the most part, was a very nice man. From the day I met him, from the day I caught him doing zumba. Only when I saw how he behaved with the kids did I start to fear him, too. And it was only the kids that he was mean to– always scolding them for making noise outside our houses. The children were always victims to the bizarre accusations brought about by the old man.

He had bought two fish, months ago. Philip was so proud of owning them. He kept them in a cute glass bowl, the bottom decorated with colourful pebbles and a tiny house for his fish. Philip often carried the bowl with him and walked around the street, claiming that he was taking the fish for a walk– and that they needed to see the world sometimes, too. It was adorable of him.

Then one day, he came out of his house, angry. Unfortunately, the children playing just outside his house were his next targets. The kids must have run to their homes in tears by the way they got scolded. Philip said to them, "Because of you faulty lot, my pet fish died! You are way too noisy, it was simply too much to bear for those delicate creatures. Now, shoo!"

It was hard to think that this man had kids of his own. Even *grandchildren*. I wondered, then, how he would have treated them whenever they visited. Of course, they would've grown up. Maybe one of them was of my age.

In the next page was a woman, smiling just as wide in her picture. Something about her face brightened my mood. She did not resemble Liza *at all*, but the vibes they gave off were the exact same. Friendly, motherly. Amanda Thomas, her name read.

"Who is this?"

"That's his wife. She passed away before I was even born, so I don't know much about her, except that she started the 'Midsummer Night's Dream' tradition in our town. She was a great drama enthusiast. To her luck, everybody was fond of her idea."

I read exactly what Flora had just said on her page. Below her name, in a handwriting so pretty, it looked printed.

I couldn't hold it anymore. The urge to just flip to my page. As much as I wanted to get to know the residents and their pasts, as much as I wanted to find out who stayed in my house before I did, there was a big curiosity to find out what was written about me, overpowering the former.

I had asked Aaron not too long ago the same question about the ex house owner. I stood next to his stall, gobbling the brownie I held like I hadn't eaten in a year. At that point, I had to start worrying about my health and wellbeing. Two brownies per day definitely seemed like a regret in the long run, but who cared, right? The quality of the brownies he made never reduced. The smell, on top of it all, made it harder to resist.

"Aaron?"

The boy in question had made up his mind to ignore me, I guessed. He pulled out a new piece of brownie and stuffed it into my mouth, breaking my record of the number of brownies eaten per day. It made me sad. Where did the new year Barkha go, who created a resolution to maintain her fitness?

"I appreciate the brownie, but why are you trying to dodge the question? If you don't know who lived there, you can just say so. I get it, it's hard to learn the names of everyone in town. I barely know fifty names, and I've spent some time here."

He still did not respond, raising my curiosity to its highest level. What *was* with him?

"Welcome, Mrs. Smith. What would you like to have?" Aaron smiled warmly. Had I become invisible to him?

I decided to let him be once I saw the crowd at his stall and suddenly at the mart too. I had to run back to it.

At the library, I sat on a seat made from jute. Since it was night time, the place was at its perfect aesthetic. Dim lights, but not dim enough that one would not be able to read. Flora had grabbed another seat right next to me, unintentionally peeking at the book I held– even if she went through it more than a couple of times already.

I flipped the page till I reached a woman I had not seen before. It made sense for me to not have seen her, but what made me keep the page open for a while was that there was also a leaving date. In December, exactly one year before I came to the town. This lady was a member of the theatre club, the same that Louis was part of.

"Is this her? The woman who previously lived in my house?" I couldn't help but ask a clueless Flora.

"What? No, she lived beside me. She's a great person. I was so sad when she had to leave town, but I sometimes still call her. Leave that, did you… come here to look for a specific person? If you did, I can help! Where do you live now?"

"The house is sandwiched between Philip's and…Liza's ex-house," I replied.

Flora's head flew back in shock. Her blue eyes could not find their way to mine, her pupils dilating. Why was she behaving like that? Had she seen a ghost?

"I…have to get back to work," she said to me. We were the only ones at the library. I was her only customer then. All the books had been arranged correctly. What work did she have?

"Flora, please tell me what all of you are hiding from me. I'm *dying* to know!"

"I don't know what—"

"There's my favourite little niece," a voice interrupted us.

Chapter 25

"I met your cousin yesterday at the library."

"Who, Flora? Good, congratulations."

"Sara, do you know that you have fans?!" I jumped off the billing counter in order to not disturb Dot. He slept a lot for a young man with healthy bones.

Sara looked up at me from her tablet, her face turning red. She tucked strands of her hair behind her ear dramatically. "So I've heard," she said.

Aaron came from behind her, pushing her head on purpose when he walked past her.

"Aaron, Flora is a huge fan of yours. She told me herself," I informed him. His ego– already over the roof– went a bit higher as he shrugged so nonchalantly.

Oliver sat next to Sara, looking into her tablet and giving her suggestions to improve her dresses casually. He had a lot more knowledge in fashion than I thought he did. Obviously, his experience as a model had taught him a lot.

"Why is she even going around and telling everybody that she's my cousin?" He asked, annoyed.

"Oh, she didn't. Your dad did."

Oliver's head shot up to look at me. "My *dad*? *He* went to the library?"

The previous night, Arch had stopped in his tracks when he noticed me. I stopped and stared at him, too. We both stared at each other and it went on for a while before he broke eye contact. Arch walked to Flora and handed her a plastic cover.

"What did you get me again? Why do you keep spoiling me, uncle?" She groaned. "Wait…donuts! Thank you thank you thank you—"

Arch chuckled. "Quit it. I know how tough night shifts are."

He shifted his gaze back to me, bringing his finger up slowly to point at me. "I…have seen you, right? Are you one of Oliver's friends?"

I nodded. "Yeah, I came with Sara and the guys the other day to pick up furniture…"

"Right! Yeah, I remember. Well, it's nice to meet you like this. Are you the girl protecting her? Thank you, that's very sweet of you."

I winced. How would I tell him that I just came to do my own research? Well, that was nothing I had to be awkward about. But seeing that there was no 'girl' protecting Flora at that time of the night, I had no heart to tell him the truth. Working till midnight was scary— no matter how safe the town was.

"Don't put her in the spotlight like that," Flora defended me…or diverted his attention. One of those.

"I'm not—"

"Uncle, don't you have to leave now?"

Arch looked offended— clutching onto his heart. "Don't send away your uncle that easily! I came here to read some books as well."

"*You* came here to *read?*" Flora asked in shock.

"Why are you so surprised? I thought I would start a new hobby." He looked at me and smiled sheepishly. I wanted to run away from this awkwardness. Who was I to be there while an uncle and his niece had a nice conversation?

He walked into the library, disappearing into the shelves as he said that.

Flora tapped on my shoulders. "I'm sorry for all that. I didn't mean to put you in the moment. Actually…my dad and uncle were worried about me staying out late. So, I lied to them. I told them that there's someone who takes care of me, who protects me. I'm just sorry you got into it. You can go now, if you want. Or, stay. It's up to you. Of course, I can't decide for you."

Oliver laughed out loud. He fetched himself an apple– unwashed, bacteria filled, dirt covered, from the fruit section. He pulled onto the sticker put on the apple and spit it out, the sticker falling straight into the dustbin. While I cringed at his hygiene, he raised both his hands up in victory and kicked his legs in the air. I looked away as soon as he took a bit bite of the apple. Sure, all the fruits there were fresh from the farm. I knew there was no bacteria or dirt whatsoever, since the fruits had arrived that day itself. It still gave me an ick. I was always taught to wash them thrice before eating them.

"That little pest, already lying to uncle and my father. She's just like me," he said, though at that moment, I did not think that was something one could be proud of. "Did you leave her, though? When she asked you to? That would've been so cruel."

"No! I didn't. How could I? I stayed with her even after your father left. She was cute."

"Yeah, whatever. She talks a *lot*." I had noticed it too. I guessed it was because she was nervous with a stranger, but apparently she just spoke a lot.

Aaron sat in front of Sara with a hand on his chin and sighed. "Sara, at this point, why don't you just get into the tablet?"

His question was very obviously meant to be rhetorical, but Sara beamed.

"I wish! I could design these dresses in 3D and they would turn out *much* better."

Sara had been more determined than ever those past few days. Why? She had given herself a deadline. She knew, only designing the dresses and not doing anything with them would get her nowhere. She had to earn money by herself. To open a shop of her own, she needed *clothes*. It had been two months since she quit her job, and in those two months since she quit, she worked harder. It was either through resentment towards her ex-manager for spreading false information to every other person he knew, or it was through resentment towards herself.

It was definitely the resentment towards himself. He had figured it out not long ago. Mahen did not see any other reason. Someone he wanted to meet, someone he wanted to be with for several days, was right in front of his door. His wife was right there, but he shut the door on his face. He didn't understand what was wrong with him. She had come back with the consideration only a God could have, come back to a murderer, and he had the nerve to shut the door and himself away from her? His wife didn't get it either. She knew he suffered. She knew what he had done, but she was ready to forgive him. For he had done all to protect her. To protect himself, and to protect the entire nation. She hated everyone but him at that moment, for running away from him. Right when he needed them the most. The same people lived in luxury under them. They did not realise that they were the hens that those cruel people raised with so much luxury, only to end up cooking and eating them later on. His people were the chickens. Mahen's people. He had tried to shoo the humans away, but a chicken needed its owner. If the humans were happy, and the chickens were happy, who were really the ones suffering?

"Barkhaaa! Barkha Barkha Barkha!"

My eyes forcefully tore away from the screen. I turned to look at a panting Sara, entering from the main door. I was not irresponsible enough to leave the door open as I immersed myself into writing. In fact, I was responsible enough to hand over a key to my closest friend in case of any emergency. Judging by her expression, it wasn't one.

"You won't believe it!" She shrieked. She jumped in the air plenty of times. Poor Dot happened to walk her away, and she accidently stepped on his tail.

"Meow!" The cat complained. Dot had grown tremendously in two months, it had surprised everybody. How could a kitten, smaller than a hand, have outgrown *two* hands?

Sara, too happy to pity the cat, picked Dot up too– spinning it around with her. Dot was smiling, I swore I was not seeing things.

"Can you tell me what's making you jump so much?" I giggled.

"You won't believe it," she repeats. "Tomorrow!" Sara said one word, and ran out of the house. Was she mentally ill?

I ran after her– this time actually abandoning my open house. A normal cat would have used this opportunity to run away from home. Not my Dot. He was as crazy as we were, running after me. To a passerby, we looked like we were playing tag. To a robber, it was a golden chance. To cats, Dot looked like a strange creature. To ourselves, it looked like an over-excited Sara running to nowhere, being chased by a confused Barkha, being chased by an also over-excited little cat, who thought everything was a game.

She only stopped when we reached the center of the town.

"Are you mad?" I asked her while panting for my life. "You made us run *this* far and for what?" It was approximately one kilometer away.

Past Barkha would've loved the long journey, she wouldn't have been complaining.

Sara picked Dot up and held my arm with her other hand. "Come, you have to look at this."

There it was– the same property the two of us had checked out before. Except, it looked a lot different. When we had seen it, it was pretty much a mess. Papers everywhere, sign ripped out, the smell of old paint still lingering. But that night, it was fully covered with beige and white paint to bring out its elegant look. A beautiful sign decorated the top of the front door. '*Incanto*', it read. A golden moon took the place of the 'C' in 'Incanto'. I could make out the existence of several hangers with outfits hanging from each one of them.

"Tomorrow, I'm opening my shop. I'm so incredibly happy right now, you don't understand!"

"Sara…" I exhaled. "You do not know how proud I am of you right now." I pulled her into a big hug, crushing Dot between us. The cat loved it.

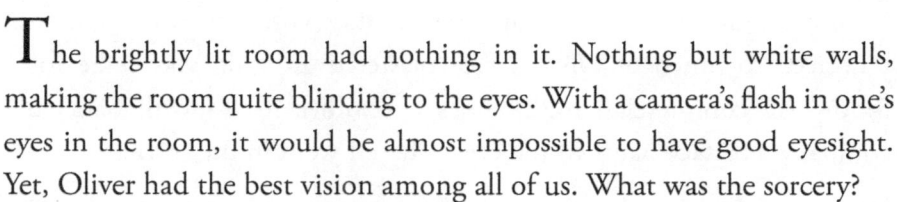

Chapter 26

The brightly lit room had nothing in it. Nothing but white walls, making the room quite blinding to the eyes. With a camera's flash in one's eyes in the room, it would be almost impossible to have good eyesight. Yet, Oliver had the best vision among all of us. What was the sorcery?

Oliver, after attending his course on modelling, gained more popularity among brands that existed in and near the town. I never would have imagined Oliver to be taking me to another town, just for me to watch him model. It was something I wanted to do, but I didn't think he would actually listen to me for once. "You have nothing to do, anyway."

He was right. Sara had her entire family helping her with the preparations. Aaron forced his sibling clan to bake cookies with him, for the grand opening…since Liza was no longer in-charge of it.

I would have sat at home and rotted while the whole town buzzed around me if it weren't for Oliver. In that sense, sure, I was thankful to him.

Oliver so gracefully and effortlessly posed with a shoe in his hand for an advertisement for a shoe brand. I watched the monitor as the cameras captured a video of him sporting a pair of shoes, turning 360 degrees and leaning backward with a sweet smile. His professionalism was at a whole different level. The boy caught eyes with me plenty of times during his shoot and did not flinch. If I were him, I would have burst out laughing.

He had never spoken about his career in detail. I was curious about many things. How did the brands get to know him? How did they scout him? How were they so confident that their products would sell better if Oliver modelled with them? How was Oliver so firm about his decisions on which brand to accept and which to not? If no brand was calling him, what would he do in his free time? He certainly would not be posing in front of the camera every single day for different brands.

In the first month of my arrival, after I had explored the town in depth, I noticed so much of Oliver's face plastered around. May it be for a toothpaste commercial, milk, shoes or clothes itself– with Sara's old company. His face haunted me everywhere I went in the town.

"Done! Thank you so much, Mr. Weiss. We'll wrap up for the day. You may all leave."

I felt everyone around me shuffling from one place to another, all either relieved and lazy to take long and fast steps, or running home in a hurry. Oliver had a foolish grin on his face when he finally approached me. "How was I?" he asked.

"You were *good*," I told him truthfully. I was not going to sacrifice a compliment for him just because I would have liked to tease him about the shoot. He was genuinely very good, it was hard not to give a compliment. Maybe because it was my first time witnessing a real shoot, but I was super hyped about it. Oliver noticed it too.

He itched his forehead, smiling shyly. "We should get back to the town. It's a big day for Sara."

"Barkha, come here for one second," Sara called out. There were minutes left before she inaugurated her shop by cutting the red ribbon tied in front of the door. I was surprised that they had the tradition in Australia, too. I thought it happened only in India. Then again, I wouldn't have been surprised if her mother made her do it.

I rushed into one of the trial rooms, dodging the body of every family member of hers. Those were not the same ones I had met during the puja on Sam's birthday. They weren't from India, they were far from it. They all had blonde hair and greyish-blue eyes. It was crazy how similar they all looked. *Any* stranger could make out that they were from the same family. I asked Sara how they were related to her, trying very hard to not point out the obvious differences between their appearances.

"My dad's mother's side. She's from Australia," she revealed. No wonder Sam moved to Australia so quickly and easily. He must have been familiar with the place. It was his native, after all. That's why I could make out foreign features on Sam. I had always wondered where he got them from. But, Sara had no gene from her Australian side, save for the accent– if that even counted.

Sara stood there with a billion hangers hung all over her arms, as if they were bracelets or the friendship bands the kids used to flex so much about in India. "I need your help." She looked at me from the mirror desperately. "I don't know what to wear…" she sighed in exasperation.

"Sara, seriously? You have a few *minutes* before everyone comes! Are you selecting your dress now?"

She tutted at that, dismissing me with a wave. "Okay, mother. I was busy with the preparations. I'm the owner of the shop, at the end of the day," she beamed. "Wow. I love saying that. Now, choose."

"Whatever you're wearing right now is perfect," I told her. Plus, it was something she had designed on her own. An ocean blue ankle-length sheath dress was what she wore. I adored the slightly puffy sleeves that the dress bore.

Sara thought otherwise, judging by the disgusted expression her face displayed.

"What is wrong with you? This is something I wore casually. There's a reason I was wearing it all along, god." The one thing I didn't understand was her reason to be pissed at me. What wrong did I do?

"Okay, sorry," I apologised nonetheless. I was *not* ready to face her wrath on that busy day. "Wear the white dress. It suits the store's aesthetics as well."

I was so thankful that I didn't receive any scoldings whatsoever for the selection of the dress. Instead, I received an encounter with the door when she slammed it on my face.

Sam was glaring at me when I walked back to the center of the store. *'Why did you make my princess of a daughter angry'* was what he was probably thinking. I wouldn't know, because he didn't say a word. He simply walked in the opposite direction as me.

With everyone rushing to help in whatever they could find, it was hard for me to do the same. Like ants, her family had crowded the store. My only exit stood there– shining and begging me to use it.

Aaron welcomed me when I opened the door. Correction: his legs did. He had passed out flat on the floor when I had opened the door on his face. It wasn't him I was worried about…the fallen boxes of cookies concerned me more. I rushed to pick them up on Aaron's side. He smiled hopefully and held his hand out to me.

"Idiot, who asked you to carry these many boxes?" My hands reached the boxes' instead of his, wearing off the smile on his face instantly.

"I hate you so much," he groaned as he got up. "First, you'll knock me down fully. How could you even do that, when the door is literally *transparent*? Do you lack cells in your brain?"

"Stop exaggerating, I was too focused on my thoughts to look up at the door. Come help me lift these now," I said to him. He helped only after a few minutes of complaining about how women were always so… I didn't remember the word he used. Neither did I pay him any attention. To everyone's relief, the cookies looked unharmed.

"Make way, make way!" Someone screeched. Upon the seriousness of the voice, every passerby split to form a path in between, except Aaron and I– who still stood holding the cookies like our lives depended on them.

Oliver had his hand in front of him, his other one near his ear as he walked carefully. Behind him was Philip, laughing and enjoying the act of a bodyguard that Oliver was pulling.

"You can stop now," the creases near his eyes deepened.

Oliver took it further. "Everyone, welcome the chief guest of the day! Mr. Philip Thomas! Welcome, welcome, sir."

Though he was addressing Philip, Oliver was stealing all the spotlight with his act. Everyone in town adored him. He closed his hand into a fist and held it close to Philip's mouth. "Tell us, sir. How did you make time out of your busy schedule for this event? Was it perhaps because you were swooned by the money the rich man gave you?" He asked so carelessly.

Both the men in question gasped loudly. Sam went over to where Oliver stood, pulling his left ear hard.

"Ouch, ouch! I'm sorry," he chuckled.

"Fool, I didn't give money. Think before you talk," Sam Arora scolded him light-heartedly.

It was Oliver's turn to gasp. His hand switched positions from Philip to Sam. "Well, sir, Mr. Philip is a respected man in the town. He made his way here and cancelled all his important meetings. And you are saying he is not worth a dollar? What gives you the confidence of revealing it to everybody?"

Everybody had given up on him by that time, all focusing on their own small talks. Sam smacked the top of Oliver's head and walked away with Philip, holding his hand so tenderly.

"What gave you the confidence to act like a fool in front of everyone? What gave you the confidence to take all the attention away on my day?" Sara had come to where the three of us stood. She didn't mean what she said, anyone who knew her personally would have known that. Her sense of humour was simply so plain and boring, people would actually assume that she meant whatever she always said. I knew not to take any of my friends seriously from experience. A certain someone had told me that whatever I had said to her then was offensive and had made me regret my words to her for a week before she spoke to me... only to tell me that she was joking and was just busy.

"The fact that I am the face of your brand, now. The male face, at least. I hope. I hope I am capable enough to be chosen by you for this. You can be the female face as much as you want to," Oliver smiled at her.

"Wait a minute... Does that mean?"

"I broke the contract with your old company. Not only was your boss really annoying, the company also did not pay me enough for representing them," he nodded.

All of our smiles dropped at the same time. It wasn't that he had made a bad choice by leaving, at all. However, he also had to consider the pay that Sara could be able to give while he represented her brand, before he broke the contract. Sara was the most flustered at the sudden news.

"But...when? What? How? Wait," she muttered to herself. "Oliver, first of all, I would love to make you the ambassador. I had always wanted to, in fact. I did not, because another brand had already stolen you. Are you sure you want to do this with me?"

Oliver's smile widened. He held both sides of Sara's shoulders before shaking her body aggressively. "Sara... I might have thought a lot before leaving your old company, but I did not have to think even a bit before I knew that I wanted to join you and your brand. I've seen your designs. You know, the quality of that company has been reducing since you left. Trust me, this is what I want to do."

I loved that Oliver and Sara could help and depend on each other when it came to their careers as well. I envied it at the same time.

Chapter 27

"Oh my god, oh my god, oh my god!"

"Come on, already!"

I glanced at Sara, my suspicions rising. "Sara…" I started.

She walked around her newly opened store in pride. Though she always mentioned that her store only sold chic clothes— more of the business type, there were a variety of clothes around each corner. She had designed up to a 100 clothes of different sets. Tops, dresses, shirts, pants. You name it— everything was available. Sara hummed without looking at me, too busy dusting off the clothes that had no dust on them.

"Are you sure these kids aren't behind you for your…money?"

She widened her eyes, finally turning to me. "Can you lower your voice, mate? They're right there!" she exclaimed.

The students gathered near the dresses section, gushing over each dress. Although it was hard to believe that it was the dresses that the girls gushed over. Someone next to me seemed to fluster them more, and the fact that they were in their favourite celebrity's store, too.

"No, I'm serious. What else do they see in you?"

She glared. "Shut up. The right question is what *don't* they see in me."

"I agree. Your ego is too overpowering that no one can see anything else. It's unfortunate."

Sara went towards her customers, waving me off. "Tell me when you're done with your baloney. Also, I wanted to speak to you about something. Meet me later."

It was not an ideal place at all. An empty basement in an empty, old mall. Spiderwebs hung from each corner. The paint of the walls dark from dust, and chipped. One could get away with a crime so easily in the abandoned place– there was no sign of residence around it. Why would Sara have chosen that place just to talk to me? The fact that I was alone creeped me out more.

I knew it was Sara, but my heart grew heavy when I heard the sound of shoes.

"You could've taken me to the cliff of a mountain and it would be less scary," I scoffed.

"You think it's scary? I think it's perfect."

I ignored her, the only thing in my mind being how safe the ground was to sit down. My doubts were cleared when Sara walked to the edge of the basement and settled there. I hated it even more since we were in the first floor. The height was an unnecessary factor that added to it being extremely suspicious.

Sara tapped next to her.

"What is so secretive, that you want to share it here?" I asked her finally.

"I wanted to tell you something..." She fiddled.

"Oh, really?" I nodded slowly. "I didn't know."

"Listen. I don't think you should continue to work at the mart," she said– just like that, with no warning.

"Sara, what?"

"I know, you need the money to live. You've told me that a million times." She sighed, swinging her legs over the ground that looked worse than the first floor. "But you aren't interested."

"Sara...please don't start again."

She turned to me, hurt evident in her eyes. Though I did not understand why she would be hurt in any way. If one of us had to be, it should've been me. I should've felt bad about Sara continuously telling me to focus on my writing, when I was very well managing both.

"What if I told you that I would financially help you until you publish your book?"

I took a deep breath before speaking. "Do you even know how absurd you sound right now? Listen, if you want to fire me, do it. I'd just find another job elsewhere. Do not try to

convince me to simply sit at home and do nothing but write. Also, do you really think that my book will sell well overnight?"

"You don't know that! I just really think you should be–"

"I'm not leaving, if that's your reason of sending me away. Sara... I know how hard it was when Aaron left the mart. Now that David left, too..."

Mr. co-worker, the day before, started a conversation with me for the first time ever. It left me in shock. "I'm leaving," he had said with a straight face as usual.

I flinched at his voice. "You're leaving what? Mr. co-worker, you know you cannot run away from here–"

"I am leaving this town. *With Sara and Sam both knowing it.*" He scowled at me.

"Wait a minute...then were you letting *me* know?!" I shrieked.

Mr. co-worker huffed a 'whatever' and walked into one of the aisles.

"Mr. co-worker! I will miss you!" I had shouted after him.

At the abandoned place, I stood up and held my hand out for her. "You don't know what you're talking about. Come on, we'll pretend this never happened."

"Barkha…"

"You're short on staff."

Sara's reaction was immediate, throwing her head back in surprise. "What?"

"Sara, I know that you have no one else to take over your supermarket. I am the only employee left," I told her.

"How did you know?" Sara's gaze dropped to the floor as she shuffled her feet.

"The first day. The 'hiring' sign. The fact that it was fully managed by Aaron before me. Now that I am the only employee, without Aaron or David to assist…you have no one else to hire. Isn't it obvious? Listen, if you let me go, the mart might be closed *forever*. You know it very well, too!"

"Maybe for the better," she replied in a low tone.

"For the *better*? Do you hear yourself as you say that? What would happen to the customers? There's no other supermarket nearby. What would happen to Aaron? You do know that he is dependent on the mart for his stall, right? So is the mart, on him. What do you think would happen to him once the mart shuts down?"

Sara remained silent.

"But…your writing, Barkha."

"I'm almost done with it, anyway. I am not going to let you give up something you had great memories of, this easily. I will continue to work here, Sara. Whether you like it or not."

Sara expressed her discomfort, yet didn't utter a word against it. "Thank you," she yielded. "But only until I can find another person to take over your spot. You don't need to worry about money."

"Shut up," I said to her, "the only thing you will be paying me for is me being an employee in your supermarket. Once I leave, I won't be taking your money."

"We'll see." She hugged me tight. "Thank you for understanding."

"Of course. I know how much the mart means to you. It solely belongs to *you*. It's the first gift your father gave to you when you turned 18. You've been taking care of it for six years now, and eventually grew attached to it. I know, your eyes were shining when you told me this."

She giggled. "Yeah, well. It is special to me. But so are you. If you happen to change your mind, do *not* hesitate to tell me."

I groaned. "When did you become so cheesy? Leave me alone."

"Thank you, Barkha," she smiled.

"Now that you're done, can I ask you a question? First, let's get out of here. Please."

The cars sped around us, contrary to the day I was there alone. With no one but two tourists and one cruel animal.

"This is where it bit you?" Sara held her stomach in fear it would disappear because of her laughing so much.

"Can we leave?"

"Barkha, how could you not know what a possum looks like?"

"In my defense, the ones I saw on National Geographic were *way* different. These creatures…do they only exist in Australia?"

Sara held my shoulder, finally recovering from all the laughter. "Still, you should be happy that you encountered a possum. If it were a kangaroo…"

"Hey, that's what Isabella said!"

"Who?" she questioned.

"The doctor that treated my wound. The same lady that I went with to watch Louis. Oh, her husband was there too."

She nodded and drove away from the place.

"Why weren't there vehicles at that time?" I asked her.

"Today, there's a famous sale going on in the next town. Everyone is speeding off."

"And if one of them escapes the town with a car that Sam owns and never returns? Would he file a complaint, then?"

Sara eyed me. "Trust, Barkha. My father has trust on the people he gave the cars to. They are all nice. If one of them happens to do so…well, the tracker still remains in the car for employees."

"Don't you want to check the sale out?"

She scoffed, hands on the steering wheel. "Why, do you know a baby? This sale only sells baby products. You know how expensive they are in the town."

"You're telling me that all of these people are heading to a sale for *baby products*?"

"As I mentioned, the products here are expensive. Also limited. If someone sold products at a much cheaper rate, which mother wouldn't rush the way these people are?"

"I am sometimes concerned for your townspeople."

"The townspeople are fine as they are. Do you want to get down now? I know a place."

"You always do," I pointed out. I opened the door to the car, anyway.

Sara sat down at the same spot the possum had bit me. "Come on." She pulled me to the ground with her. "Be glad you aren't wearing jeans or a short dress right now," was the last thing she said before my face met the grass, and then the sky again. And then, the grass. I was rolling down the slope and from the corner of my eye, I caught Sara doing it too.

"Sara, are you out of your mind?!" How many times I had asked her that in the month, only God could count. It wasn't my fault that she was *insane* when it came to many things. "When I told you that standing at the cliff of a mountain would have been less scary, I did *not* mean it!"

I had landed straight on my butt while Sara perfectly landed on her feet. Had she perhaps done it so much, that she mastered it completely?

"Look in front of you before you speak."

In front of us was a field filled with grass that were so tall, it reached our knees. Daffodils as yellow as the sun decorated the plain grass, adding colour to the otherwise boring-looking field. But... I didn't think Sara brought me there— no, *pushed* me, to show me flowers and grass. There must have been more to it.

I squinted at her. Sara let out a laugh, guiding my head toward the field again. "Do you not see them?"

Sure enough, I noticed a movement in the grass. The grass crunched, the flowers diminishing with it. The creature behind the destruction was none other than the animal I most feared to encounter there. Why was Sara doing that to me? First, she brought me to an abandoned place. Next, she not only pushed me off a cliff, she also brought the big animal with her. To anyone's eyes, it looked the same. She was trying to get me killed.

"A kangaroo?! Sara!"

Her hands flew to my mouth, covering it to prevent me from shouting. She was planning to suffocate me, too?

"Don't! You'll scare them away. Look," she made me watch the animals. The kangaroo stood still– staring at us the same way we did it. It drove me insane how it made no movement whatsoever. Like, either attack us or run away. Why make one feel anxious and on their toes when you just stare them in the eye? Though, I found it kind of cute as well, I wasn't going to lie. The way its small hands hung in the air. The way... It had a baby in its pocket! No wonder Sara had referred to the sole animal as 'them'.

"It's not a kangaroo, genius. It's a wallaby. They're from the same family, like quokkas, but they aren't the same. A kangaroo is much taller and slimmer. Wallabies are harmless."

The animal did look bulkier than an average kangaroo.

"This is the second time you guys are doing this– telling me of an animal I haven't even heard of. How many more animals are hiding in the grasses now?"

"Oh, plenty. Under the grass, there are burrows of a family of wombats. There are many birds here, too. If you're lucky, you can catch an emu walking around. But only if you're lucky."

I gaped at her. "What, is Australia a whole zoo?"

She chuckled. "Yeah, well. We're known for our animals."

The wallaby, with its baby, walked for a long time around the grass–chewing on them occasionally but mostly just destroying the flowers. Did it have something against flowers? We watched it disappear into the tall trees soon after.

Chapter 28

Sara let a pebble jump into the water, it hopping three times before finally sinking into it. She celebrated with her hands in the air. "See how good I am? You have so many things you can learn from me, yet you choose to be helpless all the time. It's pitiful."

"Oh, like leave your shop unattended on the first day? I already learnt that from you."

She sighed. "How many times do we have to go through this? Today was just the inauguration of it, and everyone could get the first look. That's the reason I had kept it open only for 3 hours. Plus, your mart isn't unattended, it is simply closed for the day. There's a difference."

"I still don't understand your system. You gave me a day off on Saturday."

"And today is Saturday," she smiled at me as if I was dumb enough to not know a simple fact.

"Sara, there's no one managing the mart right now. There's a difference," I mimicked her.

"Don't be dramatic. There's another one right in the center of the town, and everyone has a car to get there. Now, ask me whatever you wanted to ask me."

I did not want to admit that I had totally forgotten about it. I wasn't one to blame– amidst all the baby products, wallaby, pebble chaos, how would I remember to ask her?

I knew I had to ask Sara, if not anybody else. She knew the whole town. Thanks to her father, she was aware of those who came and those who left.

"Who lived in my house before I did?"

She froze. Just like Aaron had. Her face hardened and her jaw clenched. She was angry at the thought of them. I knew she was– months with Sara had made me understand the meaning behind all her expressions.

While Aaron had cowered away, avoiding the question fully, Sara seemed to be fixated on the question. She would keep thinking about whatever made her angry even if I changed the topic. What was the use, right? I decided to remain silent instead.

"Jane," Sara uttered.

"What?"

"The woman who lived in your house. Jane. I loved her, everyone did. She was a great dancer in our town. We had a whole event that was dedicated to her, only a dance event. She wasn't just famous in our town, no. Everyone in the city next to our town knew her. They all loved her, but there was a limit to the love, right? Sometimes it just so happens that a celebrity starts to get old... and boring. The people start to focus on younger artists, better ones. They completely forget about the previous one, like they were overly used socks. Things turned around for her when she started to lose the fame. Gradually, she was turning into a madwoman. Our town adored her the same, despite her insane state. So many of us went to her house to comfort her. We wanted to make her believe that we acknowledge her existence and that we're always proud of her, you know? The day she stole the town's oldest artifact and ran away..."

Sara stopped talking altogether. What she had said was enough for me to connect the dots. A town's artifact told the entire story of the town. Countries keep them in museums. People struggle to take care of their personal artifacts. I saw how close-knitted the town was. I saw that they cared about their past the same way they cared about their present and future. I saw how they loved the town's Swedish origin. Certainly, an artifact would have been so special to each and every person in the town. It being stolen by a loved dancer made everything worse. I understood Aaron's uncomfortable reaction. I understood Flora's flustered face. I understood Sara's anger. Someone had stolen something that wasn't theirs from the start and very selfishly.

"What was the artifact?"

"It was the town's most treasured possession. A rare gem we dug up when we first settled here, forty years back. It sort of held the hope of our people. Right from when they had started to live here from scratch. It had the sweat of all the people that helped dig it out. It held the story of each and every person that entered the town first. It... embodied the town's spirit. Losing it had always been our worst fear."

"So is her page in the record book? Jane?"

Sara winced when I said the name. How betrayed would every person have felt, for her to be reacting this way?

"We ripped it out. We didn't want to associate her with our town at all."

He ripped it out. All of it. The letters, the agreements. His heart. The fake care that the late Sir Monte showed towards him. The memories with the people he knew he was no longer going to be able to enjoy life with.

"Mahen..." A voice always called out to him. It wasn't a person, at all. Who would have dared to go near him? His wife had given up also. She had knocked continuously for three days on the house and gone away. Maybe forever. Maybe for the better.

"Mahen..." It called out again. It was his mind. His mind was playing tricks on him. For, in the end, his mind did need some fuel for itself. Mahen's negligence for food did not help it function better.

"Mahen..." He was overthinking about everything. That was why his brain was exhausted, he figured. He needed sleep. He needed quiet and peace.

Quiet he had. Plenty of it. The streets were deserted. Not one could step out when he did, in fear of Mahen doing something to them as well. Like he was some virus that no one needed.

It was peace that he begged for. Who else did he have to beg? Who remained, who listened to him beg helplessly? Who else, but God? A God he was beginning to doubt even existed. If he did, why did he not come to Mahen's rescue. Mahen had done all to protect his people, had he not? Had he not taken a stand amidst the cowardly?

"Mahen! Mahen!"

He forced his red eyes open. "Shut up!" The walls echoed his shout.

"Mahen, please! Open the door!"

It was not his mind. It certainly was not. His mind was not as nice as the voice sounded. His mind was cruel and taunting in nature. It mocked his existence day after day. The voice that called out to him instead was laced with hope.

"Mahen!" It called again. This time, it was a voice too familiar for him to forget.

It made him sprint to the door as fast as he could. It took Mahen a minute to reach the door, and all his energy was used up in the process. He hated it so much, yet refused to eat anything.

His wife's body met his puny one when she gave him a tight hug. "Why is your skeleton showing?" She showed her concern towards him. He didn't pay it any mind. All that mattered was that she was back. She was back again, and did not look like she wanted to leave. The caution that was miserably masked by a thin expression of joy that she had carried during the previous attempt to return did not exist anymore. She was easy to read into and so was the feeling of discomfort. What was the point of Mahen allowing her to live with him if she were always on edge around him?

His wife had thrown all the anxiety in the bin before she came. Her brave and courageous nature had welcomed him once again.

It took a minute for Mahen to acknowledge the presence of not one, but many. Behind his wife stood all the people that ran away from him. All that feared him.

He stood there silently, his confusion very much evident as he observed them. On their faces was not fear, not anger, not disappointment, too. They bore a sense of faith, a sense of hope that ignited in them. Mahen then realised that they weren't there to fight him, they instead looked up to him in whatever way.

"Mahen, please forgive us. It was our foolery to hide from you. You are our hero," one of the elderly said.

"You are our hero! You are our hero!" The people behind him repeated.

He wondered if it all were but a fever dream.

"Mahen bhai, I am only a farmer. I suffer with little to no food a day. That cruel lot took away all my happiness. All my hard earned crops are gone, bhai! The only thing that remains is indigo. What am I to do, what am I to do!" One spoke from the crowd. He wept into his hands in sorrow.

"Dada, I am a handicrafts man's daughter. Our shop is forgotten. They took down all our businesses as well, dada! The heartless bunch did it all. We are all so troubled," a young girl followed.

The same elderly man— the leader of the clan, spoke up again. "We know now that they are only looting us. We owe you a huge apology. We now understand the nature of your sacrifice."

"There's no need to apologise," Mahen said, his eyes moist. "We have all had our chance to be mistreated, exploited by them. But, we shouldn't simply give up. We won't spare them until they go back to their own country."

"We won't spare them, we won't spare them!"

Mahen's voice, he realised, had grown more powerful and filled with conviction, thanks to the support he had received. He understood that a tiny squeak from a mouse could turn into a roar of a lion within a minute's time.

A sense of patriotism, understanding and a sense of unity lit up within each person present— like a series of matchsticks. The flame in Mahen's heart was flaring up, no matter how shattered the heart was.

Chapter 29

"People always ask me how I come up with song ideas while I write for the group. What if I tell you, I barely think about the ideas? No, I am not a born genius that the ideas just come out of nowhere. Of course I'm using my brain while making the melody or writing the lyrics. I hate to say it out loud, but I am not a perfectionist. I don't look at how perfect the lyrics are, or how flawless the melody is. I just start writing, letting my subconscious mind provide the ideas to me while I bring it on paper. I think the most genuine songs come out of spontaneity. It's called incubation– the phase where an idea suddenly occurs to you when you step away from the problem.

To all the writers– whether it be for songs, stories, books, or even news– do not force yourself to sit and write. And I cannot stress this more. It will only end up giving you results you never wanted. Bad quality, like the law of attraction.

It's okay to be away from writing, trust me. The world isn't going to end if you don't write once a day. You can take your time– walk, watch anything at all. Sleep, eat. The ideas strike you at the random-est of times."

I took a right abruptly, startling a poor child crossing the road. The car stopped to the side as I pulled out my phone. "If you want to send comments or questions that you want me to answer, you can send them at..."

I was already at it. "Hey, a regular listener here. I always wondered if your songs are from your personal experiences, because I seem to relate a lot. I don't really know why… there's just some kind of resonance in me with Cinque's songs."

"User 0065 says…"

My hopes were raised unnecessarily.

"'Hi! I love your music, I really wish I could attend your concerts!' Well, I'm not going to reveal anything, but be prepared for one in Sydney soon! I did reveal everything…didn't I?" He let out a sheepish laugh.

"User 0107 says 'I would like to formally apologise to you. My pet parrot is butchering your song now.' Hey, don't demotivate an aspiring singer. Okay, I'll read one more before I close for the day," he hummed a song. I pictured him scrolling through his phone, searching for comments that caught his eye among a million others.

"Okay, last one. 'Hey, a regular listener here. I always wondered if your songs are from…"

Wait! That was *my* comment! I sat up straight and my hands on the horn accidently pressed it too hard. I should have been grateful that no one was on the street anymore.

"Hmm…interesting. Are you one of the members? Yes, I take inspiration from literally my whole life, and the members'. I try to convey their experiences into songs, that's all I do. They play a major role in my songwriting process. And if I were to talk about my personal experiences… yes, **'Sparkle'** is an inspiration from my childhood, **'Chatter'**, as you all know, is about our member fights. I have plenty of experiences quite literally turned to songs. I'm glad you can relate to them! But also, if you happen to relate to the sad ones, I pity you…"

I did relate to the sad ones as well. The ones about writer's block, about feeling lonely and out of place, about having internal conflicts. But that was not something I had to be worrying about at that moment.

I happened to glance at the watch on my hand and freaked out. It wasn't the mart that I was late to. No, I had put up a sign that read ' We'll be back at 3 p.m.' clearly in front of the mart.

I informed Sara about it before doing so. She told me, "go, get your book!"

I knew nothing about the publishing process in the town. Heck, I didn't know about it in the whole country. My friends had absolutely no idea as well. It honestly shocked me. Oliver and Aaron, I could understand. Their jobs had nothing to do with what I was looking for.

Neither did Sara, for that matter. But what really differentiated the kids were their parents. Sara had *Sam Arora*. He was practically the town's leader. Philip and the other elderly were nominal executives. Sam, though a real estate tycoon, did know everything about the town– including the best publishers. As his daughter Sara should have been subjected to learn from her father. "Stop, I don't even know what I ate for dinner last night," she replied when I questioned her.

With Liza no longer around, I had to resort to my last option. Which naturally was the best one. Jimmy Brown.

Jimmy Brown was not only a published author but also a very down-to-earth man. When I had enquired about the publishing through phone with him, he suggested we talk about it in person– in his house.

There I was, greeting and thanking Jimmy for the hundredth time that day.

"I haven't done anything for you yet, and you're already thanking me?" He smiled.

Mrs. Brown was just as welcoming. She conversed with me in her posh Aussie accent. If I wasn't lying, I found the accent very hilarious otherwise. She could have been the only one that bore the accent and made it sound understandable and luxurious as well.

"Here," I handed a thick file to Jimmy Brown. "Sir…I respect you immensely. You are the first one I'm showing my book to. Please feel free to give me your honest feedback. Your feedback matters to me the most, here."

He let out a laugh. "Of course. I will be completely honest about the story. Come, drink some tea with me as we talk about publishing."

I did not care to switch the radio on while I returned to the mart. It was pretty useless, since the voice in my head would have been louder, anyway. I thought back to what he had said to me, wondering if it really was the best option. Of course, there was no doubt that Jimmy was a highly respected author. His suggestions changed the whole idea I had planned out in my head.

My mind had decided on that morning, soon after waking up— I was going to talk to Jimmy and he would give me the numbers of all the publishers he knew. I would shoot my shot in each one, and would simply hope that at least one would accept it.

He had turned it all upside down— toyed with my brain with the new concept he referred to.

The image of him sitting with crossed legs and sipping on his tea still sat in the front of my head. "Barkha…why don't you try self publishing?" For some reason, he seemed hesitant to bring up the topic. Did he know himself, that it was not a term many people heard?

I had no idea how 'self publishing' was even done before he introduced it to me. I always thought it meant printing our book and all its thousand copies by ourselves— in a printing shop.

"There are many websites in which you can publish your own book."

Upon asking why he didn't recommend me going to a traditional publisher, he sighed heavily.

"You know, I had made the mistake of being trapped under a publication company all those years. Self publishing is but a new concept. Back then, I had no other option. They take away all your royalties, dear. I agree that they deserve a major part of it, but the companies in the town are no good. They scam you into believing that they're the best company to exist and that they'll make you famous. You may receive popularity, but for a book you didn't even write. Because the company would have edited many things you wanted to keep in the book. Then, they take all the money. They tell you that they did most of the work and so they deserve it. We receive less than 2% of royalties, when 10% should be ideal."

I was still contemplating on self publishing. I knew that traditional publishing would get me to reach more readers, for sure. But with all that Jimmy mentioned, I wasn't exactly leaning towards it.

Another thing that was on my mind besides the publishing was the book itself. Its ending. Would he like it? Forget Jimmy, would anyone like it at all? It wasn't one they might expect, neither was it one they would particularly enjoy.

The Sun was up that day. Brightly it shone, and everyone rejoiced. Finally, the terrible days of extreme rains were over. The Sun was back to greet them— happier than ever. The Sun wasn't the only cause of the people's happiness. The day was a day everyone came out of their houses— irrespective of their religions. The entire city would be lit up with lights. Diwali, Mahen's favourite festival. The elderly woman ran around to each house— feeding each person a sweet that they prepared the previous night. It was one day that the men would get to relax in their homes instead of working, but they choose to help in the decoration of their houses.

Mahen was extremely happy. He had his wife, he had his new born baby. Though he barely got to see his own baby— the baby was snatched away by the women of the area, who always adored it and looked after it as their own.

'Veer', Mahen decided to name him. It meant bravery, or a warrior. It was exactly what his father wanted him to be.

"You have such a lovely child," one of them cooed at the baby.

"Look at his dimples!" Another exclaimed.

The children of the area often made a pit stop from running around just to admire Veer. They would get scolded by their mothers when they attempted to touch his cheek. "Your hand is dirty! Do not touch the baby. Go play, now."

Mahen watched all happen with a proud smile on his face.

As the sun dipped, the lights only grew brighter. Mahen was with the children, teaching them to light the crackers.

His heart dropped when he saw light. It wasn't regular light like the ones lit up. Several green lights on torches were up, travelling all the way to where he stood. He knew then.

The sound of boots got heavier as the seconds passed. They marched together, faces holding a firm expression. Mahen could do nothing but stare as they neared.

His people were already screaming. His wife ran to his side with the baby, holding it for its life.

He knew there was no point in rebelling against forces that already had his life in their hands. When they held both his arms and dragged him away, he showed no signs of sadness or resistance. His calm act surprised the whole lot of people that stood to witness the happenings in tears.

He didn't question anything. Mahen only wondered how it did not happen earlier. The metal cuffs on his hand hurt less than the wounds in his heart.

At the court the next week, he felt like a showpiece in a museum that everyone stared at, as the judge uttered his final statement. "I have made my decision. You, Mahen Singh, are to be sentenced to death by hanging."

His execution was something no one wanted to look at, though they couldn't tear their eyes off the body of a real warrior as he hung– hands cold and blue, neck gruesomely accessorized.

The soldiers had disappeared, heartlessly killing the criminal in his own village. Only his people stood to watch him. His wife had locked herself in her house with their baby.

Mahen's statue stood tall in the centre of their village. One he wouldn't ever be able to see. His people smiled widely, remembering the times they enjoyed with the man. In a world of darkness, his legacy was continued. That in itself rose a beacon of hope and light in the darkness.

"What is wrong with you!"

"I'm sorry! Is it bad?"

"What *is* wrong with you?" She questioned again.

I stood at her counter while she did not even face me. Her eyes were busy scanning the clothes that had arrived newly from the tailors. She compared one dress with another– deciding which would go where in order to attract customers.

Although she didn't need to make an effort to attract the customers. I was not referring to her father being famous, no. Neither was it her fame with the youngsters. Her shop genuinely did catch a lot of attention because of its interiors, and the variety of clothes available. Even those that weren't from the town had to stop by before passing the town.

The familiar ringing of bells was heard as both our heads shot up to look at the customer. A low pony, colourful clips decorating her hair like a fairy from an animated book. Flora was back, and very much lived up to her name with the floral dresses she often wore.

"Hello," she passed us a shy smile and disappeared into the hangers of clothes.

"The ending!" Sara shrieked, probably startling the poor girl too. She turned with a sudden movement, her hands placed on the counter in rage. "Why would you make me cry?"

I couldn't help but laugh at that. "You, and cry? I never thought that would've been possible!"

"Barkha, *you* made it possible! Don't you understand? I loved your book so much."

"I'm usually a slow reader. Actually, I don't read. Your book was the first one I couldn't keep down," she continued.

"I'm so relieved. Now I just wait for Jimmy's signal, edit it once more and I'm ready to publish it. I already checked a website that can publish it as well! It's way cheaper than I thought it would be."

"You don't know how happy I am for you," Sara sighed.

"What about you? How's your shop going?" Sara and I hadn't met in *weeks*. She couldn't come to the mart while I worked because she owned a shop of her own. It was not like she could abandon it at any time. After work, I went straight home to work on the editing of my book— adding new chapters that extended the story and could make the readers build a strong connection with Mahen, removing unnecessary chapters.

"I really need someone that could help me. I can't manage a shop alone, especially when customers flood in and have so many questions for me all at once."

"You can hire me!" Flora came in front of us with a squeak.

Sara looked at her up and down, judging the girl. "Flora, you're sixteen," she pointed out.

"I turned seventeen a week ago. What does that have to do with anything? You know about my passion for designing– Oliver told you. Plus, I'm no longer in school."

As soon as the academic year was over, Flora had left it. She told me on a Sunday night at the library. She knew she wanted to do anything but study. Her parents were extremely supportive. It made me wonder if they did so just because they suffered financially. But it wasn't my business to dwell on it.

"They no longer need me to work at the library…the manager returned. Please? Let me show you what I'm capable of."

Flora had an extraordinary sense of fashion. It must have been in their blood. She dressed in a way in which her only competitor in the town was Sara. Sara knew, too, about it. She openly admitted it.

"I already know what you're capable of, Flora. I just…"

'You just what? Are you hesitant because of my age? It shouldn't be a worry. I come here so much that I memorized every item you sell and where they are located."

Sara smiled at her. "You're cute. Fine, you are hired. Start working here from tomorrow."

With a squeal, she hugged Sara all of a sudden.

Sara pushed her away, yet she held a smile on her face. "Stop it, kid."

Chapter 30

"I...I..." Jimmy Brown stuttered. "Barkha, I have no words to describe how your book made me feel. The emotions I felt as I read through the entire book. I laughed and I cried. Mahen is truly...amazing, if there's one word to describe him. I loved your story so much. You *need* to publish it."

I had taken Jimmy's advice after much consideration. I had no idea if the book would reach any person, save for my friends and neighbours. Sara and Aaron promised to stick posters of it around their own stalls or shops. Oliver told me that he would tell everyone he met about the book. I couldn't have been more thankful to receive friends like them.

I had tears in my eyes as I held on to the hardcopy. Freshly printed. The pages still crisp. It was unreal...whatever was happening. Many months ago, I entered the town with new hopes and dreams. The fact that the same dreams had come true, collectively bonded into one book, made my heart flutter as I ran my fingers through the soft cover.

Louis, with his great interest in books, was the one to rush into my house to read the book. Dot stood, his hair standing up as he hissed at the young boy.

"He hates you," I said to Louis.

"He hates my lovely cat Snarkles," he corrected.

"He hates you."

Louis had been a foolish boy to bring his cat to Dot again when he grew up. "Dot was a baby when it met Snarkles. Now, they will get along with each other very well," he had said. I was more foolish to believe him. Cats weren't like us humans. They had a much longer memory term. Louis and I should've both known it when Louis came to visit us in front of Dot.

Though he didn't seem to care to get along with my cat the way I cared. He only wanted the book that I wrote.

"Zenith," Louis read out the title. "What does it mean?"

Zenith. The highest point of something.

The title resonated with me when I looked up the meaning of it. Mahen's bravery to face the colonists was at its zenith. Mahen's power was at its zenith. Mahen's *struggles* against colonial oppression was at its zenith. Not only Mahen, but his people, too.

Louis was out the door before Dot prepared to jump on him in an attempt to attack him, confusing the poor cat.

I found myself walking back to Sara's shop instead of the mart I was supposed to be at. I had to be grateful that Sara did not yell or even glare at me for entering her shop and disturbing her. The last time I had gone, I was brutally kicked out for talking too much by the owner herself.

She embraced me when I entered. "Congratulations!"

I thanked her, but she was not the one I was looking for. I walked over to the young employee, who remained fixed on her work– placing the new arrivals on hangers. I tapped her for her attention.

"Barkha...hi! I heard about your book being published from Sara, congrats!"

"Thank you," I said to her, "that was why I came to you. Do you know if the library you worked at accepts readings? Like, I will read parts of my story out loud to whoever can attend it…if they do. But do you think the owner of the library will allow that?"

Flora's face lightened up. "Of course, she will! You don't have to worry about that. She is a huge fan of books– if that wasn't an obvious fact. She's amused by new writers, and the ones that aren't as famous as the others. You do not need to ask twice for her to agree on the idea."

Flora gave me more confidence than I expected. So much so that I was already on my way to the comfort place. I had been to the library after Flora left, yet I made no conversation with the owner. We simply exchanged smiles whenever I came in. I read, and then I left.

The woman looked up when the door opened and smiled like usual. Except, she was a little taken aback when I walked to her and waved.

"Hello, I'm Barkha…I guess you could say that I'm new to the town. I came a few months back."

"Oh. Hi, dear," she said awkwardly.

"I actually published a book that I wrote," the second I said that, her attitude toward me changed. All the awkwardness of talking to a stranger had disappeared, and a new sense of connection built inside the two of us.

She was the first stranger to read the book. I was beyond terrified to hand it over to her. I was more so to watch her reaction.

She called me one day, while I worked at the mart. "I need to speak to you."

And so there I stood– the only one nervous in a pool of happy faces in the library. The librarian, Flora, Sara, Oliver and Aaron. We all watched as people occupied the seats, all with expectant expressions. With each person entering, my anxiety increased. The way I had felt in the bake sale was nothing compared to the way I felt in the library.

I had the librarian assuring me that it was very good for a debut novel. I cleared my throat before starting to speak to the people present there.

About twenty people sat and stared at me as I started to read a small chapter of the story.

"...And Mahen listened to Sir Monte, because that was always what he did." I stopped reading and examined everyone. Jimmy Brown sat in the last row, smiling up at me.

I introduced myself right after. Two or three walked out of the library without saying a word to me. I was disappointed in myself, for sure. Though not so much when the majority of them directly came to the shelf that displayed dozens of copies of my book and read the back of it.

One man told me, "The voice modulations you made with every sentence was amazing. You ever considered being a stand-up comedian?"

Another young girl said, "I'm going to finish your book within a day! It sounds so interesting. Congratulations on your publishing!"

I spoke to people I never had spoken to before, when Jimmy Brown approached me last. "Barkha, you did amazing. I'll buy a copy right away!" he laughed. "Also, I'm not sure if you want to go, but there's a literary fest happening next week, where new writers can display their works in their own stalls and a hundred readers visit each stall that interests them. I would strongly recommend you to go with this book. You'll get a lot more reach than you already are."

Chapter 31

I found big similarities between the bake sale and the literary fest. Both were held outside, both had a million stalls that the visitors could check out. The only difference was the topic of the events and the two being held in different towns.

As I set up my stall, I observed the ones next to me. The one on my right– a stall covered with spider webs and huge spiders hanging from each which I was hoping were fake. A bright red light inside the stall despite it being morning added to the effect. It was clear that they were selling a horror book. The one on my left– in contrast– was filled with flowers of all colours, hay lying on the ground. The person inside it wore a hat made out of straw, smiling widely at anyone who passed by her stall– whether they were interested in her book.

I had stuck snippets of news even I couldn't read, because of how old and worn out they were, to show that my story was placed in the past. Toy guns hung as a set on top of the newspapers, right next to where my books were put. I definitely did not aim for it to mean 'take my book or face the gun', although that was a good way to put it. The idea struck me as a man walking by commented on it. "Are you going to kill me if I don't read it?" He had laughed, yet even under the threat he simply walked away without giving the book a chance.

If I were an audience, I would have found it all too exciting. Only the thought of roaming around a ground filled with stalls of different themes, different stories explained by the authors themselves...it felt like heaven. I didn't get to feel anything but anticipation when I stood inside. Was this what running a business felt like?

The lady with the horror themed stall visited mine. "G'day, mate! What do you have here?"

Unlike her stall, her personality was bubbly. She went on and on about how fun all of this was— that she had published her debut novel, too. "Everyone told me that I'm too old to switch careers now. But, who cares, right?" She laughed out loud, holding her stomach as she did so. She styled a bandana on her head, her hair frizzy and yet stringy— apparently matching the style of the protagonist of her book.

"Wait, we were supposed to match styles with our protagonists? Where will I find a moustache and a hat, now?" I cried out.

"You don't have to," she chuckled, "if it were a compulsion, the boy at the stall in the end would have dressed up as a donkey."

I thought that keeping a donkey as one's protagonist was very strange... until I found out that it was only a children's book. Otherwise, what would he write? 'Hee-haw, hee-haw'?

Quite a lot of people visited the stall I stood in, a few bought it, a few listened to me and moved to the next one. I wondered if it was because my book was not relatable to the people of Australia since it was about the Indian struggle. If it would sell bigger if I were in India.

During my lunch break, I checked out every author I could. I bought a lot of books I thought were interesting, already excited to read and take notes on the writing style of each one.

"That is just the introduction," I said to the people. "If you read my book, you'll gain a deeper understanding of what I actually mean right now."

"This seems interesting, eh?" A girl whispered to another, probably thinking that I couldn't hear her…when the two girls were the only people in my stall at that moment.

"I don't know. I better start looking at other stalls. We're running out of time!"

"I'll stay back. Meet me at the entrance after an hour," the first girl told her.

As she looked at me, I straightened my back and cleared my throat. Her energy was so strong, I had figured out that she was one to speak out loud and open.

"Hello, ma'am. I'm Ava, a social media influencer. I have a fair following on Instagram– almost a million, to be exact. All I do is promote and review books. I found yours, especially, a good book from what you explained and from the back of the cover. Would you mind if I posted about your book, too? I reckon there's a bunch who'd love the story."

"I…of course! It's a big honour for me, ma'am!" My voice came out louder than I expected it to, catching the attention of the horror lady. She simply peeked in for a moment before going back into her own, displaying no expression.

Meeting Ava was one of my biggest accomplishments in my life. A big influencer putting up a post for anybody was a huge deal, especially in a time where the youth were pretty much living for their phones and social media. Ava asked if I could put the book on an online market for everyone to be able to access it. With her guidance, I did exactly that.

Was I too blindly following the advice of someone I did not know one bit? Yes, but at that point I was too fixated on the number of people reading the book to care.

Her camera did all the work– dragging her hands with it to capture every part of the stall before focusing on the main character– the book itself. I was not surprised that she did not show my face to the camera, but the fact that she did not utter a word in the video was unexpected. Or I was too much of a 'boomer' to be thinking that way. I wouldn't know.

"You just have to wait a week or two, ma'am. Your book will be reaching heaps of people."

I had returned home with a proud smile on my face and a few boxes lighter from the bunch of books I had sold out. Outside the mart, I noticed a poster as big as one's face hanging right where everyone could see it– unlike the poster wishing to hire someone– marketing my book better than I did myself. Aaron, busy with his work, could only pass me a cheeky grin when he caught me gaping at the poster. "I put it on myself," he said quickly. I was forewarned about the posters, but I had thought it to be a joke and got over it. Little did I know they were far from joking.

Literally.

Every corner near my house had at least one poster, the same one, regarding my book with the library's address. I teared up from all the support I was receiving, even from the young boy Louis. If only Liza had been there so I could share my enjoyment with her.

I sat on the same bench I had with Louis when I first got to know him. "Congrats, Barkha!"

"For what?" I asked him.

"Ava posted you!"

I quickly rushed to open the social media app for the millionth time that day. "I've been checking it for the whole day, and she decides to post it only when I'm not with my phone," I huffed, speaking to myself because

Louis paid no mind to me— indulged in watching a bird peck on grass, which seemed more interesting apparently.

"Oh my god," I breathed out as I stared at the screen displaying the influencer's face.

"I told you so," Louis smirked. It wasn't the influencer's post that I was amazed at. The numbers next to the heart and the thought bubble caught my eye.

"A hundred thousand likes…"

"Check the comments," he told me.

'I love the storyline! I'll have to buy the book now'.

'Where can I find this book?'

'I've read the book, it's beyond amazing.'

Wait…*read the book*? My head shot up to look at the boy. His gaze was already on me, anticipating my reaction.

"That's my comment. See how many likes the comment itself got! Ten thousand!"

"Oh Louis, you're a sweet boy. Thank you."

Chapter 32

"I went home the other day and asked Noah how my radio was that day. You know what he told me? He told me that it was starting to get *boring*. The nerve of him to say that!" He chuckled. "So I called him here. Literally, he's like– right next to me. I told him, 'let's see how well you can host a show'. Noah gave me a new idea, though. A new segment I could start. I would act as an interviewer every Thursday. I would get famous people on the show, and talk to them as casually as I can. Won't that make the show interesting, Mr. Noah?"

For the first time, I was able to hear another voice on the radio. He said, "I guess so. But I still think it would've been better if you just handed the whole radio show to me. It would get more listeners."

AV repeated his words in a tone that mocked the other. "Whatever makes you sleep at night. Guys, should we just send him out right now?"

"Okay, okay. I'm sorry," Noah laughed just as I parked my car.

My feet guided me through the dark alley when I let my eyes scan every shop on the way. I had my suspicions that it wasn't a place one could trust to begin with. My mindset towards the place had changed when I saw Arch's shop, believing that every other shop owner was similar to Arch. Though, something about the alley convinced me that innocent shops were not the only shops that existed there. Would I get money if I reported an illegal shop to the cops?

In a month's time, I had overcome the fear of roaming in the alley. I still refused to go in the night, that was a different thing.

As much I hated it, Oliver's house was located in the same alley. He just never mentioned it to me.

Since he told me that his grandfather had enjoyed reading the book I wrote, I had gotten a lot more comfortable in going to his house. There was no one to judge me there, after all. His grandmother often invited the three of us for lunch. I kind of felt bad for the number of times I accepted her offer without a thought. While she probably enjoyed our company, I had to consider her age…but I never did, too blinded by my love for the food she prepared.

I always scolded Oliver for having the nerve to eat outside when a cook like his own grandmother existed. Forget Aaron, and even Liza, for that matter. Oliver's grandmother was incredible in whatever she cooked.

His grandfather opened the door for me. Their house was not big like Sara's, or small like mine. Amidst the shops in the alley, their house was the biggest property.

"There she is, my favourite author!"

It still amazed me how it had already been a month since my book got published, and since the post that basically gained me more readers. It wasn't like I had a huge fan following, or anything, that someone would stop me on the road and say, "Aren't you the author of Zenith?" No, the townspeople were more familiar with *me* than the book. They knew I had published a book, and congratulated me whenever we crossed paths. I doubt they read it.

The one thing that made me so grateful to Ava was that my own followers on Instagram had gone up by a thousand.

"You look like a fool, standing there and staring at nothing," Oliver said to me while munching loudly at the dining table. The other two also ate with him.

"Wow, you started off without me?" I scoffed in disbelief. None of them cared to answer that.

Sara and Aaron, both on their phones, didn't look up to greet me. While Aaron laughed at whatever he was watching on his phone, Sara wore a much more serious expression while scrolling.

Oliver's grandmother served me her world famous lasagna that I heartily enjoyed. "Look, none of these talk to me anymore," I complained to her, pointing at three of them. Oliver stuck his tongue out at me like a little kid.

"Ignore them. I'm here for you," grandma said, her words coming out a lot sweeter than I was expecting– unintentionally touching my heart.

"Oh my god guys, you won't believe it," all three heads looked up at me when I said that, making me wonder if they were really there for me or for the everyday gossip session I entertained them with. Working at a mart had its own advantages. A mart was where the customers were relaxed, not minding about the employees listening to them. The things I had happen to hear from people while they shopped was…interesting, said the least.

"Today, at the mart I met a woman–" My sentence was cut off by my own phone's rings. Who would have been calling me at that hour of the day?

"Hello? Am I speaking to Barkha?" The voice on the other end of the line said.

"Uh…yes, but may I know who this is?"

"We're calling from Sydney Scene Channel. We have read your book, Zenith, and we thought it was a very good book. We would like to interview you, since your readers are increasing every day. Could it be made possible?"

My heart stopped. I did not mean to let out a gasp, but I did, and ended up embarrassing myself in front of the caller. My friends were all curious– Sara continuously signing for me to put the call on speaker.

"Wow…yes! Of course! I'm available anytime. Yes! Thank you so much."

The three of them were so close to me when I had cut the call, all gazing at me nosily. I told them, and Sara scrunched her eyebrows.

"I have never heard of the channel. Are you sure they aren't trying to scam you? Google them first."

It turned out that 'Sydney Scene' was as popular as any news channel in Australian TV. The mail they sent to me online confirmed that they weren't trying to impersonate the channel, either. It was real. The channel. The interview. My book.

"Sara, don't act like you know," Aaron lamented at a bashful Sara scratching her neck. Her expression immediately changed– she glared at Aaron, the glare strong enough for him to remain quiet.

"Barkha…look." Sara handed her phone to me. On the screen, a post with several location stops and dates beside them. The account that posted it– Cinque.

"Concert dates," Sara clarified my doubts. "But look at the date beside Sydney. They match perfectly."

Sure enough, the seventeen was when they were performing at Sydney– they first ever stop in their tour. My interview was scheduled for fifteenth.

"If we can buy the tickets, I'll come with you to Sydney. We'll stay there for a week, explore the city, too. It'll be both of our first times there," her excitement reached the roof.

My smile widened the same way hers did, our chests rising in a feeling we couldn't contain to ourselves. The boys had no interest.

"But the mart…" I sighed. Sara realised, too.

"And the shop…"

Sara exhaled. "Do you think Flora can take care of the shop alone…?" She asked with hesitance.

"No. She's still a child," I told her. "You can't leave the whole shop's responsibility to her."

"Well yeah, I know that…but Cinque!" She exasperated.

Aaron chimed in, patting my shoulder. "I'll take care of the mart for a week. It isn't a big deal. Plus, my oven's been acting up these days. I can't keep the stall open even if I want to, for now."

Oliver nodded. "Fine. I'll be there with my little cousin at your shop, Sara. I doubt I'll be able to spend a whole week with her, but I'll try my best."

"Wait, don't you guys want to come to Sydney too? If not for the concert, you could look at it as a trip," I turned to look at them.

"Maybe another time," Oliver said and Aaron agreed to it. "I have work here now."

None of this made any sense to me. Right from the call, to the concert, to Sara. What was happening was unreal.

I thought about it and realised that Cinque had spoken about interviews in their radio show only minutes before I got the call for the interview, too. It showed how connected I felt to the group, or AV himself.

Chapter 33

"Are you going to take a year in there?"

"Shut up," I said, hugging my cat.

"No, if you are, then let me know. I might as well be productive right now." I rolled my eyes at Sara's constant nagging, knowing that she couldn't see me.

"Oh! I think my hands broke from carrying all the luggage!" Sara chimed.

"I haven't left Dot like this, for so long."

"I love Dot, but he's a *cat*. He can survive without you."

I spent a lot of time thinking about who I should give the cat to. Philip was not an option to begin with– he was allergic to cats. Louis was blacklisted by the cat himself. Oliver was terrified. Aaron couldn't trust his own siblings with Dot. Liza had gone, unfortunately.

It took me a lot of courage to give him to Flora's care. Her house or family information, I had no idea of. I almost went back to the record book in the library to find out, or rather guess, how well they could take care of Dot.

"You have a lot to say for someone who *insisted* I keep this thing," I lifted Dot in the air like Rafiki did Simba.

"I told you to keep it, not make its life miserable."

"Dot, don't listen to her," I blocked the cat's ears.

Sara hated being late to anything. It was a quality of hers that I really liked. The problem was, I was the opposite. I was always late to the most important events. Sara found that out on my first day at work, much to my luck.

She came two hours early to pick me up that day. Curious, I had to ask her why she never went to a Cinque concert when she could go anytime she wanted. "I didn't have friends who enjoyed the music. What's the use of going to a concert alone? I would rather listen to them on the radio or on my phone," she replied.

The airport was at the extreme end of the town, Sam's office very close to it. Going to the same place reminded me of the time I had entered the beautiful town, with zero expectations from the townspeople.

The airport gave me the same nervousness and excitement that it did almost a year ago. With Sara that day, the only emotion I could feel was happiness. Her presence contributed only a little to my happiness— most of it coming from the interview I was going to Sydney for.

Sara did not match my mood in the aeroplane. She would've been excited in her mind... So excited that she fell asleep the minute we started to fly.

"You're no fun," I told to her.

"Have you ever considered looking within yourself first to know why I'm not fun around you?" Was the last thing she mumbled.

Apart from having more buildings and lesser trees, Sydney wasn't much different from the town. In fact, it wasn't that different from *India*, either— save for the people and their accents.

As clichéd as it sounded, we had to visit the Opera House on our first day there— even if I insisted I stay in the hotel room and prepare for the interview that was happening the next day.

"Come on, don't be a spoilsport. You can sleep less at night," Sara, giving bad advice, dragged me out of the room.

The place was filled with tourists. I knew that because each person looked of a different race, all wearing hats and sunglasses like a regular tourist would. I might have seen a couple Indians, too.

Sara ran around each market in the long street filled with food. We gobbled up the gourmet sandwiches.

"Ma'am, can I have one mo–" my mouth was covered by Sara as soon as I said it. She shushed me, saying, "We have a million other stands to try!"

We eventually split up– she was more interested in the food, while I was dying with my stomach full. I sat on a bench near the food market with my notebook open. My eyes mindlessly scanned the page. Before travelling to Sydney, I had made a list of the things I was going to say in the interview, but it was of no use– during it, I would stumble over my words anyway.

I made the foolish mistake of tearing the important pages, assuming I would only be carrying them with me and not the book itself. The pages were stuffed inside the book, so I carried the whole book everywhere I went. What was really the point of tearing the pages, I had no clue. So when I removed my hands from the pages to grab my phone, they all went fluttering away with the wind. I looked dumb enough to the locals there when I gaped and gasped at the smallest of things, but when I dropped the papers, everyone looked at me with a weird stare.

I bent down to pick up all the pages when someone walking by stamped on it.

"Hey!" I objected, lifting my head to stare at the rude person. A man rolled his eyes at me from above. He and the person beside him both wore masks and black hoodies, most likely to cover their faces. Were they thieves?

My eyes shifted to the other person– very familiar in appearance. The same pale face, the same blue eyes. My doubts were cleared.

"Wait a minute… *Tristan?*"

I guessed that he smiled under his mask, giving me a little wave behind the rude man's shoulder.

The other man scoffed before walking further, stamping the papers again– intentionally or not, only he knew.

"Hey!" I repeated, much more offended. "Pick these up!"

Tristan held his shoulders, taking him with him. "Sorry about that," he muttered under his breath. I followed them, continuing to nag at the man.

As they went away, I could hear the man's voice for the last time. "Who's the crazy girl following us?"

I stopped in my tracks at that. "Excuse me?" I shouted, but they were long gone. All that remained were dirty sheets of paper, me and the locals that glanced at me. Was the man Sara's long-lost twin? Why was Tristan so distant, when we had met after a century? Why did he look somewhat… embarrassed? My questions were left unanswered.

With unsteady steps, I entered the building. It was huge in comparison to the tallest building in the town. Maybe, even taller than the hall that hosted Isla Everly's fashion show.

'You must be Barkha, the author of 'Zenith'?" The woman behind the front desk asked me.

"That's me."

She led me up the elevator and into a room similar to the one I watched Oliver model in. Except, the white walls were covered with a big black cloth behind the two chairs kept. On the cloth– a big sign that read the name of the news channel with its logo beside it.

"Hello, ma'am. Welcome!" The lady wearing cat-eye glasses spoke. With her blonde hair, she looked like she could be Rita Skeeter's sister. It was more plausible because both of them were journalists.

I sat on the chair facing the interviewer with my hands on my knees, consciously staring at the billion cameras in front of us. With a 'camera rolling…action', the interview began– the woman beside me a lot more casual and comfortable than I was.

"Welcome back to Sydney Scene, today we are here with the author of the best-selling book, 'Zenith'! The book gained immense popularity in the past few days, and we received so many messages from our viewers to invite you to the show," the interviewer smiled at me.

"Oh, really? It's a great honour for me! I would like to thank each and everyone for reading my book and loving it as much as I enjoyed writing it."

The woman took a deep breath and nodded before continuing. It must be so hard being a journalist, always listening to people they might not even know, talking about their whole lives.

"Tell us about your writing journey."

"Well…I moved to Australia from India not even a year ago. It took me a couple of months to complete the book, but here I am. Before writing it, I had been watching a lot of movies and shows related to the colonisation in India. Mahen is completely a fictional character, but the struggles he and his people went through are very real and can be compared to the actual struggles that the people of India went through. I wanted to bring awareness to it."

"I hope it isn't a rude question to ask, but why did you shift to Australia, when you write about your home land? Does your family live here?"

I stiffened. I did not want to reveal my family problems on national television, ever. "Oh…it's because I love this country. I had always wanted to live here. I love the nature, the people, and though it's hard to admit– I love the wild animals, too. I was attacked by one!"

"Who gave you the inspiration to write?"

I laughed at that. "At first, no one, if not the actors in the movies I watched. It might sound surprising to you, even I cannot believe it yet, but I met with the author Jimmy Brown. He was the one who first inspired me to continue writing, and then encouraged me to publish the book. He was the one who read my book *first*."

Sara waited outside for me after the interview. She complimented my behaviour for the first time. "You didn't seem nervous at all."

Two days later, the two of us sat on the seats located in the back of the hall for the concert. We were too late in booking the tickets, it seemed, because the only good seats that were available were the ones three rows before the last row of seats. I was not complaining– getting to sit in a Cinque concert itself was a big deal.

The celebrity band made us wait for fifteen minutes. I nudged Sara.

"What?" She turned to me with excitement.

"I want to use the washroom…" I told her.

"Go, then."

"Come with me pl–"

"Don't even think of completing that sentence. I cannot miss their entrance."

I tsk-ed at her. "Such a good friend, you are."

She shooed me away, staring at the empty stage.

Where in the world was the washroom? The sign outside clearly showed the picture of a door that pointed to the right, but where was it? Was it perhaps inside the black metal door I was facing?

Though the band had not entered the stage yet, the screen on the stage displayed videos of the members. I heard the familiar voice of AV's, the cheers as if I was sitting in the crowd— so loud and clear. I turned away from the door to the source of the sound. Suddenly, someone from behind me opened the door— making me fall to the ground. In defense, I kicked the person's legs with mine, my eyes still closed from the pain.

"Ouch, dude, what the heck—"

Both of us went silent. The hurt I got when I fell down was long forgotten. The fact that I was in a concert was forgotten.

"Barkha?"

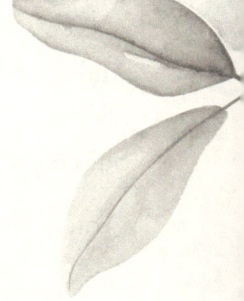

Chapter 34

Was this really happening, there? In a concert, out of all places? In *Australia*?

The boy I knew for years was standing in front of me, and still neither of us could utter a word. It was as if someone had forced us to speak, or as if we were strangers trying to get to know each other.

The truth was, no one knew me better than he did. No one knew *him* better than I did.

It was the shock that prevented both of us from moving a muscle.

"Barkha…" He repeated.

"Avi. What are you doing here?" My calm appearance was a facade, and he was well aware of it. It wasn't Avi himself who made me feel so quiet. Meeting him brought back memories of my house that I had tried so hard to forget over the months.

"What are *you* doing *here*?" He asked back. His voice had changed. Of course it had– eight years was a lot for a voice to change, but it wasn't the matured voice that I was most taken aback by– it was the accent. He spoke in an Australian accent. In an astonishingly familiar tone.

"I'm attending Cinque's concert, obviously. But…"

And then, it hit me. I felt as though a brick came swinging at me when I realised. No wonder I had found his voice familiar. Not at that moment, but before it. *Way* before it. When I turned on the radio for the first time.

"You're AV."

Was I so stupid to not guess it earlier? AV, Avi. Avyukt was his birth name, sure. But Avi was what everyone referred to him as. He simply changed his stage name to AV.

"And now welcome, Cinque!" The voice from the stage resonated strongly.

Avi looked alarmed. "I have to go now, meet me here after the concert."

"AV, man, come on!" A voice shouted from inside the black door.

"Coming!" Just like that, he walked away from me.

I could not enjoy the concert like I wanted to. The fact that I had reunited with my closest friend was supposed to make me feel happy. I *was* happy, but more shocked than happy. I barely even looked at the screen the whole time. I spaced out on the stage itself, which appeared to be occupied by ants, from the distance we were at. The hour felt like a flash. I only started to vibe with the music to the end of the concert, when they sang the first song I listened to. Serenity. The same emotion rushed inside me. The same feeling rose like a fire in my body. Euphony. Avi, I figured out, was the main vocalist.

"Where are you taking me?" Sara sighed. I did not reply to her.

I reached the same spot I had an hour ago. Sara widened her eyes at me.

"Are you *crazy*? This is the backstage room! Are you planning to stalk the band?"

Just as she said that, the door opened to reveal my best friend.

"Hello, Avi," I said to him.

He couldn't hold in the smile on his face. He pulled me into a hug immediately. I didn't look at Sara to know that she was freaking out on the inside.

"How come you're here? *Why* are you here? In Australia, of all?" He asked me.

"How come *you're* here! Weren't you in the US? Did you not want to become a pilot?!"

We both laughed, not that we found anything humorous, but just because everything was much too thrilling. Being able to meet one's best friend after years of separation and no contact by mere *coincidence* was near to impossible.

"Wow…" Sara's voice was finally heard. She glared at me and I already knew that our journey back to the hotel room was me facing hell.

"Meet Sara," I introduced her to him. "She's my dear friend from the town I live in."

Avi called out to his members. Each of them came out, one by one.

"No way…" *Again*? At that rate, my heart would fail from all the shocks I was receiving. "Tristan! Weren't you a businessman?"

He wore the same expression as me, but still smiled. "Musicians can also be considered businessmen. I didn't want to reveal myself as a member of Cinque. I didn't even know you, who knew what you could do?"

The same rude man I encountered three days ago on the streets stood next to Avi.

"You…" he said to me. That time, he had a personality completely different from the one he had at the market. "I'm sorry. I didn't know that two of my members actually knew you. I thought you were a stalker. I'm Noah, by the way. Nice to meet you."

"Like the Noah AV interviewed first?" I beamed.

Avi tilted his head at me. "You listen to the radio?"

"You even answered my question once! Oh my god, this is too much to deal with in one day."

The only other man in the band was called Charles— which was quite an old name for a man that young. He gasped when he saw me. "Aren't you the author of 'Zenith'? I saw you on TV."

"Oh my god, Barkha? You were *the* Barkha?" Avi questioned.

With precaution, Avi and I went to the farthest restaurant possible from the concert venue, in a car driven by his manager. Sara got back to the room after she forced a promise out of me, a promise to tell her the A to Z of the whole situation.

"I still cannot believe this, Avyukt."

"Barkha, you're telling me! A popular *author*, now? I've heard of the book, and knew that the author's name was Barkha. But I did *not* expect it to be you. Tell me, how did you escape from your house?" He chuckled, evidently meaning it as a joke. He stopped when he saw me not laughing. "Wait…seriously? I'm so sorry that you had to do that, Barkha."

"Meh. You know how often I spoke about running away? I actually did it a few months ago."

"What about uncle and aunty? Have you spoken to them?"

"Do you think I would speak to them? You should know me, Avi," I laughed. "Never mind that. You tell me, how did you get an *Australian* accent of all? If you had an American accent, it would at least be understandable. You showed no interest in music as a kid. How did you expect me to identify you from the radio?"

Avi explained to me how he stayed in the US for a year before his father had to shift again to Sydney. They were all settled there forever. He got into bad influence at school, then was peer pressured into changing his accent. 'Peer pressure', not because his friends pressured him, but because he himself felt out of place and changed it *for* them. It turned out that the 'bad influence' turned out to be a great one, since they were the ones who got him interested in music. It became a big passion of his, and made him start a band of his own...consisting of the 'bad influence' friends. Tristan, Noah and Charles were his friends from his school. I found it all too amusing. At seventeen, he had already met the people that practically shaped his future as well as their own. It was also hilarious to picture Tristan being of any influence at all, especially bad. From the hours I knew of him.

I, in exchange, explained to him the reason I ran away, the 'snap' that caused me to do so. I told him all about my new life in Australia– how I had many people that I could rely on in comparison to India, where Avi was pretty much the only one I could rely on.

"Barkha," he called out to me on the way to my hotel room after he offered a drop. I hummed in response, texting Sara about my arrival. "Can I invite you to my radio show? Now that I have started to interview people and now that your book is pretty much going viral, I think it would be amazing!"

I laughed at that. "'Viral' is an overstatement. But I would *love* that so much. Like, imagine being on the same radio show as a world famous band– with millions of listeners. Actually, are you sure you want to get me on? You're Cinque, at the end of the day."

"Of course I want to get you on! *At the end of the day,*" he mocked, "You are Barkha and I am Avyukt. I think the show would be the most comfortable with you."

Euphony

I carefully entered the room. A pair of hands grabbed me and shut the door, all in a millisecond.

"Whoa," I breathed, looking at Sara.

"Tell. Me. Everything."

The atmosphere at the radio show felt a lot more safe, or rather comfortable, to be in. Avi was a probable reason.

"The concert was a huge success, thanks to you guys," he started off. One thing I liked about his show was that he *never* started it with a 'good morning' or even a 'hello'. He started it with a regular sentence, like he was making conversation with a friend. It told a lot about the band's relationship with their fans. As I sat next to him, I felt a rush of adrenaline. I forgot that Avi was even my friend, the feeling of being an accomplished fan overpowering it. Knowing him as a celebrity was more recent than knowing him as a friend.

It was my last day in Sydney, and the most productive as well. Avi had invited me to his parents' house for lunch right after the show. I was more than delighted to accept the invite. Avi's parents were not as close to me as Poonam aunty was at that time, but I still enjoyed their company, and vice versa.

"Today, I'm here with someone I least expected to be here with. My closest childhood friend, who authored the best-selling book– Zenith. You guessed right, welcome Barkha!" He cheered.

"Thank you, thank you. It is an honour to be here. I represent all of Cinque's fans, I cannot believe this is happening!"

"Shut up," he smiled. "Guys, she's putting on an act right now– she was cursing at me a second ago."

"No, I wasn't!"

"Tell the listeners about your book, Miss Barkha. And then go away."

I repeated the speech engraved in my brain once again. I did not even need the dirty papers that were stepped on anymore.

"Let's answer a few questions before ending the show for the day. Oh, one comment reads, 'How close are you to Jimmy Brown?' Wait, you're close to Jimmy Brown?!"

"Yeah, I look up to him as a renowned author. He lives in the same town as I do, so we meet quite a lot, especially since the publishing of my book. His wife is someone I talk to as well."

"Wow. Okay, next question. 'What was your parents' reaction to–' yeah, let's move on–"

"No, don't move on. I'll just say it. My parents aren't supportive of me becoming an author, but I have come to respect their decision. AV and I spoke about it some days ago, and I thought about it the whole night. They have their own ideas and understandings about a career. They are not familiar with the idea of an author, or any career besides a doctor or an engineer, because that's what they have been doing, that's what their *parents* have taught them. And I understand them not supporting me till date. I only hope we'll be on the same page one day, but that's just hoping. I am fine with talking about it anywhere, I'm not ashamed anymore about having different ideas from my parents."

Avi held my shoulder with a proud smile. He showed me a thumbs up in approval before closing off the show.

I asked Sara to come along with me– she had nothing to do in Sydney, all alone.

She proved me wrong. "I do, actually. I have to meet up with someone here. You enjoy."

"Barkha!" His mother embraced me when she opened the door. Eight years, and she hadn't aged a bit. It was fascinating. "How are you, sweet girl? Avi told me about how you met."

His father told me that he read my book, and showed me the proof of owning it. "Thank you, uncle. I feel honoured."

When asked to choose between orange juice or kokum juice, I chose tea. I told them how much I missed the tea from India. Thankfully, Auntie had a whole pack of tea powder from India, understanding my distaste for the awful taste of Australian tea, of course from the POV of an Indian.

I was engaged in a conversation with both Avi and his dad when aunty came in the room enthusiastically, holding her phone to her face. "Guess who's with me, now!" She shouted at it. All of us turned our heads to her.

Aunty tilted the phone to me. My face dropped, same as the people on the screen.

Chapter 35

Avi rushed to his mother, talking to her in a hushed tone. His mother looked confused.

My eyes were fixed on the people on the screen. "H-hi," I stuttered, cursing myself for it.

"Barkha," a soft voice spoke. My mother's eyes were glassy, even noticeable from the phone.

"Hi." I was at a loss for words. Contrary to how confident I was at the radio show while speaking about them. They were as surprised as I was. Little did they know their daughter was in Australia. They had *no* idea about their daughter's location at all, before it. It made me feel sad.

"Beta, how are you?" She was crying at that point. Watching her cry made me cry too— shamelessly bawl my eyes out in front of my friend and his parents.

"I'm good, aayee," I said in Marathi. "How are you and baba?"

"We're both good. We're just missing you a lot," her voice quivered.

"I..." I hated to admit it. Correction— *past* me would have hated to admit it. The Barkha from India would be fully against me. The 'town's newbie' Barkha would have stopped talking to me. "I miss you guys, too."

"Please come back to us, beta. Please come home."

"I'll try to, aayee. I will. I have to go now," I cut the phone call even if I did not want to. I couldn't handle the emotions, so I rushed to the washroom right after throwing the phone on the sofa.

"Barkha, are you okay?" Avi's mother called out, knocking on the door. "Avi told me what happened before you came to Australia. I'm so sorry, I genuinely did not know."

I wiped the corner of my eyes, sniffling. "It's fine, aunty. I'm not blaming anything on you. I'm just…overwhelmed."

"I'm sure you are. Do you want to come out and talk about it?"

I opened the door and hugged her again, to feel the *motherly* feeling again. "There's nothing to talk about. Let's eat?"

Avi walked me to the lift after lunch. "I hope you're fine," he asked carefully.

"I am. Avi… I want to go back to India."

He looked taken aback. "Barkha? Are you sure about it? You don't have to force yours–"

"I'm sure. I've not been more sure. I want to explain everything to my parents, get a good relationship with them. But first, I'll go back to my town and say my goodbyes."

"I'll take you," he decided.

"But you're so busy, I don't want you to sacrifice anything for me."

"I'm not busy. My concert just ended, which means I get a month off. Let's both go there for a month. I haven't visited it in forever."

My steps back to the room were slow. I opened the door with my keys lazily.

"Hello, Barkha."

My head shot up to the voice inside our room. "Sara...Liza?!"

I ran to her with joy, the thoughts about my parents in the back of my head. "Liza! Oh my god, you have no clue how much I missed you!"

"I missed you, too." She grinned. "Bestselling author!"

"Stop," I denied. "How is life here?"

"It's very good, I love my little granddaughter. I love my son and his wife! Being a parent is the most fabulous feeling. It makes me miss my parents as well." I flinched at that.

"I'm so happy for you."

"Thank you, but I just wanted to meet you to tell you that I'm so incredibly proud of you for everything. You are living your life to the fullest. Barkha, you are an inspiration to me. Now, leave. You're getting late for your flight."

I pushed Sara back. "Idiot, you had her for the whole day, could you not call me to meet her for more time before leaving for the flight?" She shrugged in response and chuckled.

"You were busy. It's okay, I got to see your face again, and that itself is a big thing," Liza patted my cheek. "Visit Sydney again, you dumb kids. Next time, come home. I will show you my granddaughter."

"Of course! You visit your town, aunty. The whole town misses you."

"I'm sure they do," she smirked. "Bye, for now. We'll see each other soon."

On the flight, I told Sara about my plans. "I'm going back to India. I planned to stay there for a month, taking Avi with me."

"I respect your decision, Barkha. You're doing good by going back. Greet your parents from my side."

The truth was, that I had no idea when I would come back. Avi would leave in a month, but what if I changed my mind while being there? I had a week to spend in the town before I left for India, so I had to make the best of it.

"Why are you crying?" Oliver asked me, handing me my luggage.

"I…I will miss Dot, of course. How can I leave my cat and go for a *month*?" I lied. I would miss my cat, but the town mattered more. *They* mattered more, all of them. Old man Philip, Louis, Jimmy, Liza, Sara, Poonam aunty, Oliver, Aaron and Flora. The best of friends I had made all my life, excluding Avi.

"Silly girl," Sara punched my stomach with love (hopefully).

I turned 360 degrees for the last time, taking in the town I grew to fall in love with.

In India, I turned around with a different feeling. A feeling of hope. A feeling of a new start.

"Aayee…baba…" I mumbled, eyes worn out from all the crying. I bent to touch my father's feet– holding on to it as I cried even more.

"Stand up, beta," my father told me. "I missed you so much." The two greeted Avi.

Over tea, I told them about the book I wrote and handed each of them a copy of it. Avi bragged about how popular I was in Australia.

"Are you not disappointed?" I asked them.

"At first…we were, at you leaving. But then we realised…you mattered more than our thought on your career does. What you do should not be a sacrifice to us never being able to see you, ever. You are exceptional in your writing, from what Avi tells us. You have achieved enough– *more* than enough. We are very proud of you, Barkha." The words made me tear up another time.

Over the weeks, Avi and I made it a habit to visit every place we knew of. The lake, our old school, my grandparents' house, the beach. All along with my parents. My parents and I had built something that never existed between us, and reconstructed the old and broken bridge of our relationship. So much so that I could happily say that I felt the fatherly and motherly feeling from them, quite literally though, more than I did with Liza or Poonam aunty, or Avi's mother– even Philip, for that matter. We could openly and freely joke about me running away again, without worrying about the possibilities of it actually taking place.

We had a great time of arrival, too. Just before my favourite festival. Unfortunately, I could not see the celebration at Sara's place. Many might not enjoy the Diwali cleaning, but I loved every step of it. The sweeping, mopping and the dust on the shelves cleaned in the previous year did not bother me. Avi, on the other hand, was not to be seen. I didn't know why he was trying to get on my mother's good side when he already was adored by her... since childhood. The only time I spotted him was when I spotted my mother. She didn't mind his presence either, rather had the same enthusiasm as my best friend.

My favourite time of the festival was, for obvious reasons, the bursting of the crackers. It was as basic as vanilla ice cream, but who would not love the flower-like shape in the sky? Agreed, there was more variety in crackers– flower pot, chakra, simple sparklers etc. But our alley had an hour *just* for the fireworks. 10 in the night. A perfect time, if anyone would ask me. Post dinner and pre sleep time. Everyone could enjoy it.

It resonated with me in a special way. All the years, my family would stand together and look at the sky– wishing for things only we, as individuals knew. No one cared to ask each other what their wish was, but we made a promise to make each other's wishes come true. To not go against any wish, especially after finding out what the wish was.

"You want to know what I wished for the year before I ran away?" I asked my father. He smiled in response, putting his hands in the pockets of his khaki pants. We stood in the first line of the crowd, like we always did. If the people complained about us pushing them out of the way, my father scolded them— muttering something about reuniting with me and it being a special bonding time. No one even listened to him but me.

"You probably wished on leaving this hell of a house…," My father said.

"No," I held his hand in mine. "I wished for you guys to be happy even when I was gone. That you didn't ever have any regrets and neither did I. That none of us felt any kind of negative emotion. Part of the wish did not work, unfortunately. Because the moment I saw your faces on the screen that day… I began regretting everything. I *needed* to get to you both immediately. It wasn't even a want."

My father sighed. "What stupid firework were you wishing on? No part of it worked. Do you even know how bad your mother and I felt when we looked at your empty cupboard?"

"I'm so sorry, again. I hate myself for doing this without discussing it with you."

He hugged me tight. "You don't have to be sorry. *We* do. For treating you this way. For forcing a career upon you— one which you had no interest in. Actually, I'm so glad you know what you want to do. We would hate to see you unhappy in life. We were too blinded by our own fake happiness that we forgot to consider yours. Now, you are happy and so we are happy."

A week before we had to leave, I got a call from an Australian number. "Hello…?" I asked slowly.

"Hello, is this Barkha speaking?"

"Yes, who's this?"

"Ma'am! We are calling from Emu Editions, a publishing company in Australia. We read your book and fell in love with it. We really want you to join our publications. We have a good reputation in the market and will guarantee more than 20% royalty. Please, consider joining us. We will make you get more reach than you already have – worldwide reach."

"I'll think about it," I said, surprised by the sudden call. I immediately called the first person I thought about.

"Jimmy! How are you?"

"Hey Barkha, I'm good! Tell me, what made you call me?" He listened attentively while I went on about the call.

"Should I accept it? You tell me."

"Barkha…see. Ultimately, it's your choice. I should have no say in this at all, but if you really want my opinion, do it. Join the company. I know I spoke badly about publications, but you have already published a book. Now, you are a well known author in the literary community. You will be called for many interviews and directions in which you will receive full royalty. Emu Editions is a great company, moreover. But do as your mind tells you."

"Who called you?" My mother asked, stirring a pot of my favourite *dal* made by her.

"A publication company. They want me to join them."

She turned around with a huge smile. "Oh my, Barkha. My little girl is all grown up and famous!" I giggled.

"I decided that I would join it. But…for that, I'll have to go back to Australia."

Her face dropped, getting sadder as I continued to speak.

"Aayee, I do not want to leave you and baba. But I will have to– work calls. I promise to visit you every possible time. Trust me, I will make time to come here."

"I know that your work is important, my dear. I still do not want to let you go."

An idea struck me. "Do you guys want to shift with me?"

To my dismay, she rejected my offer. "Like you have work there, your father has work here. We have a committee here that we would hate to leave. You visiting us often is what we want."

"Okay, I understand. We still have a week together, don't be disappointed!"

In one way, I was very happy to be going back to Australia. To my family there. To my *own* committee. In the other, on the day I had to say goodbye to my family in India, I hated to go back.

"Promise me you will take care of yourself," I asked the both of them.

"We promise," they laughed. My mother rubbed red vermillion, a bindi– on my forehead. "You will be back soon, right?"

"Right. And if you ever miss your lovely daughter, I am one call away."

Avi watched the moment, his heart warm. He told me that on the airplane. "Don't worry, Barkha. I'll be visiting you, too. I am one call away from you, too!" He imitated me.

"Okay, Avi, Shut up," I was embarrassed about the stares we received from the people on the plane. Avi was fully covered up because he was a celebrity, so making a fool out of himself was not that big of a deal. No one found out who he was. I, on the other hand, wore regular clothes like a regular person– exposing myself and my face to the whole world.

The reassurance that Avi was in Australia was what comforted me. I could visit him anytime I wanted to, and vice versa. In just an hour's flight.

I had zero regrets when I stepped back in the town I belonged to.

Yes…I belonged in the town. Not in India, not in Sydney. With my friends. With my cat. With my neighbours. In Sam's territory.

It almost felt like the party that was held that night was for me, a 'welcome back, famous author Barkha!' party. It wasn't, unfortunately. It wasn't held for any reason, and I couldn't even question the town for it. Because that's how silly the town was, and the people in it.

When Sam clinked his glass– this time with me next to Sara and a different person wearing the tiara, I cried. I wished that the same fate as mine repeated for the person wearing the 'newbie' batch– looking as confused as I had on my first day there.

They welcomed the new girl, but I felt them welcoming me. I felt *myself* welcoming me. I was not scared, disobedient Barkha anymore. I was carefree, famous author Barkha. The new personality of mine was welcomed.

www.ingramcontent.com/pod-product-compliance
Lightning Source LLC
LaVergne TN
LVHW041920070526
838199LV00051BA/2682